The BIG Book of Simple Solutions™

Training Your Dog

Plus Other Helpful Tips

By Kim Campbe'

Illustrations by B.

BOWTIE PRESS®

Irvine, California

Karla Austin, Business Operations Manager
Jen Dorsey, Associate Editor
Michelle Martinez, Editor
Rebekah Bryant, Editorial Assistant
Erin Kuechenmeister, Production Editor
Ruth Strother, Editor-at-Large
Nick Clemente, Special Consultant
Michael Vincent Capozzi, cover design
Vicky Vaughn, interior design and layout

Library of Congress Control Number: 2003114518
ISBN: 1-931993-27-0

BowTie Press®
A Division of BowTie, Inc.
3 Burroughs
Irvine, CA 92618

Printed and Bound in Singapore
10 9 8 7 6 5 4 3 2 1

Contents

House-Training

The Secret to Successful House-Training 7

How Long Does it Take? 8

How Do I House-Train My Puppy? 12

It's Cold Outside. Can I Paper-Train Him First? 15

Reward Performance 19

The Benefits of a Crate 20

Preventing Potty Problems 27

What Goes in Must Come Out 29

Accidents Happen 31

Cleaning Up 35

Chewing

Why Do Dogs Chew? 41

When Chewing Becomes a Problem 45

Dog-Proofing Your Home 50

What Should Dogs Chew? 57

Teaching Your Dog to Chew Toys 63

Ways to Redirect Problem Chewing 68

Preventing a Chewing Problem 74

Digging

Why Do Dogs Dig? 79

Digging for Fun 83

Digging for Prey 89

Digging for Shelter 91

Digging for Attention 93

Digging out of Anxiety 97

Digging to Escape 99

More Ways to Prevent Digging 101

How to Deter Digging 103

Correcting Digging Behavior 109

Barking

Why Do Dogs Bark? 115

Who Barks and Why? 119

When Barking Becomes a Problem 122

Solving a Barking Problem 126

If You Want Your Dog to Act As a Watchdog 138

Be Patient 140

Bark-Control Devices 141

Puppy Preschool 147

Aggression

What Is Aggression? 149

What Does Aggression Look Like? 152

Bully Boy or Fearful Fido? 154

Other Types of Aggression 161

Who Ya Gonna Call? 166

Dealing with Aggression 168

Changing a Dog's Behavior 171

Can Drugs Help?... 178

Diet and Exercise.. 180

What Not to Do 182

What's the Prognosis?... 183

Obedience

Petiquette for Pooches... 185

Who's the Boss?... 187

The Social Graces of the Urbane Dog.................................. 188

Beauty Is As Beauty Does 195

Sitting Pretty.. 196

Jumping Up.. 200

On or Off the Furniture?.. 201

Mealtime Manners 204

Come When Called 207

No Marking Please! 211

The Eleven Commandments of Good Dog Ownership......... 217

Index... 220

House-Training

The Secret to Successful House-Training

Puppies pee. And poop. A lot and often. If you've never lived with a puppy, you'd be amazed by the number of times the little furballs need to go potty. Every hour or two, they start sniffing and circling, looking for a place to do their business. If owners aren't watchful, accidents can frequently happen.

Not surprisingly, house-training is the first lesson new owners want to teach their pups, and rightfully so: House-training is the foundation for good behavior. Without it, dogs can't become members

of the family, and they run the risk of being exiled to the backyard, never getting the attention and social interaction that they need and deserve.

Happily, the secrets to successful house-training are simple: Time, patience, consistency, and supervision are all that's needed. Puppies are quick learners. A regular potty schedule, combined with praise for going in the right spot, and they'll soon get the idea. Dogs are naturally clean animals, and they don't want to soil their living area. House-training teaches dogs that the house is the living area and the yard (or whatever spot you choose) is the potty area.

How Long Does it Take?

Just as with children, potty training a puppy is a process. It's not something a puppy can learn in a day, or even a week. While it might take only a few weeks for your dog to understand what you want, until he's four to six months old, he's not physio-

logically capable of "holding it" for more than about four to six hours. A dog's muscle control isn't fully developed, and his bladder is not large enough to "hold it" any longer than that.

Remember that each dog is an individual. Some pups are potty trained at three months, while others may not be completely reliable until they're nine months to one year old.

A number of breeds are more difficult to house-train than others, including: many toy breeds, such as Chihuahuas, Yorkies, papillons, Chinese cresteds,

Italian greyhounds, shih tzus, and poodles, especially the smaller ones; the bichon breeds, such as bichon frise, Maltese, Havanese, and Bolognese; various hounds, including beagles, Afghan hounds, salukis, harriers and foxhounds; Jack Russell terriers; and soft-coated wheaten terriers. These dogs need extra supervision and a lot of positive reinforcement.

If you acquire your puppy at eight weeks of age, expect to take him out at least six to eight times a day. By the time he's about six months old, potty trips will be down to three or four times a day. A rule of thumb is to take your puppy out in hourly intervals equal to his age in months. For instance, a two-month-old puppy should go out every two hours, a four-month-old every four hours, and a six-month-old every six hours. This can vary, of course, depending on the individual dog: Some young puppies need to go out every half-hour. It's your responsibility to make sure that your puppy gets plenty of opportunities to go potty in the right spot.

Other good rules to follow include taking your pup out first thing in the morning—yes, even before you have your first cup of coffee—and ten to thirty minutes after every meal, when he wakes from a nap, after every playtime, and the last thing at night, just before he goes to bed.

That's a lot of dog walks. What if everyone in your family works or goes to school? Those things are important but so is your puppy's potty schedule, especially for the first couple of weeks he's with

you. Without a schedule, your puppy can't learn what he needs to know. Try to get home once or twice during the day, hire a dog walker or pet sitter, or ask a friend or neighbor to take your dog out. Try taking time off work during the first week of house-training to firmly establish the schedule and rules in your pup's mind. It's helpful to start training on a weekend or during a long holiday.

How Do I House-Train My Puppy?

Start house-training your puppy as soon as you get him home. Even before you bring him into the house for the first time, take him to the potty spot you've chosen, and let him sniff around. Make note of any patterns of sniffing, circling, and squatting. These are his clues that he needs to go out. If he performs, praise him in a happy tone of voice, "Good potty!" Then take him inside, and introduce him to his special place, which can be a crate.

Dogs develop preferences for certain potty surfaces, usually based on what they learn as a puppy. It's a good idea to expose your pup to different potty surfaces such as asphalt, concrete, and gravel so that if you don't have access to grass, you won't have a problem getting him to go.

Young puppies should not have the run of the house. Before you bring your puppy home, choose a safe area of the house to let your pup stay. This is usually a kitchen, laundry room, bathroom, or some other area with an uncarpeted floor. Rooms with tile, vinyl, or concrete floors are good choices.

Lay down papers in this room (this is not paper-training but simply an easier way to clean up messes). Put your pup's open crate, a couple of chew toys, and a food and water dish at the opposite end of the room. Close off the room with a baby gate or other barrier to prevent him from wandering throughout the house. Until your puppy is house-trained, he needs to be under your direct supervision or confined to an area where he can't get into trouble.

The goal is for your pup to eliminate away from his crate and eating area whenever you aren't there to take him out. Once your pup is consistently eliminating in a certain spot on the papers, you can gradually take up the papers, leaving only the favored area covered.

If you come home and your pup has pottied in the safe room, don't scold him. He's just doing what comes naturally. Take him outside and praise him when he potties in the chosen spot. If you take him to the same area every time, the lingering scent will prompt him to go again.

It's Cold Outside. Can I Paper-Train Him First?

Most trainers agree that teaching a puppy to go on paper and then retraining him to go outside can be confusing. Some dogs never quite figure out that they are supposed to move on from papers to the great outdoors and continue to potty on any pile of papers they see. One puppy who had been reliable in the house for some time had a relapse one day when his owners were painting the hall. They had laid down papers to protect the carpet, and he came along and squatted on them for a quick pee. They hadn't paper-trained him at all, but apparently the breeder had laid down papers to protect her floors and the smart pup remembered what they were for. But if you live in a high-rise building or are unable to walk your dog regularly, try paper-training or litter box training.

To paper-train your dog, spread a few layers of paper in the area you want your pup to go. Then, instead of taking him outside, take him to the papers. Let him sniff around, but if he moves off the papers, set him back on them. When he eliminates, praise him.

If you're having trouble getting your pup to use the papers, try this trick. When he urinates, hold a sponge underneath the flow to capture some of the urine. You can then use the sponge to scent the papers. The next time you take your pup to the papers, he'll smell the urine and remember what he's supposed to do. You can also purchase pads at pet supply stores that claim to induce eliminating. When the pad is placed on the papers its scent is supposed to encourage a puppy to eliminate there. It's worth a try if you're having problems.

To house-train your dog with a litter box instead of papers, follow the same process as paper-training. Litter boxes and litter suited for puppies

and dogs who weigh up to thirty-five pounds can be found in pet supply stores. Shredded paper, which some dogs prefer, can be substituted for litter.

Reward Performance

After your puppy eliminates praise him. Choose any short phrase that works for you, and say it in a happy, approving tone of voice. When you assign a name to the action, your puppy learns to associate the word with the act and may learn to go on command. Just don't make the mistake one owner did of using the phrase "Good dog" or your pup will start going potty every time you praise him, whether you meant him to or not. Make sure everyone in the family knows the key phrase for going potty and uses it consistently. You don't want your puppy to become confused.

Speed up the training process by making potty time pleasant for your puppy. Keep some tiny treats in your pocket so you can reward him the

instant he's through eliminating (don't interrupt him before he's finished). Then, spend a few minutes playing. He'll soon learn that the quicker he does his business the sooner playtime comes. This is useful on rainy days or when you're in a hurry.

The Benefits of a Crate

Dogs are den animals, which means they like small, cozy spots such as the caves of their wild ancestors where they can curl up and feel safe. Since most of us can't provide caves for our dogs, a wire or plastic carrier, or crate, is the next best thing.

Many people don't like the idea of putting their puppy in something that looks like a cage. It seems cruel to them, but just the opposite is true. Placing your puppy in a crate when you can't be there to watch him keeps him safe and out of trouble. When he's in his crate, he can't nibble on the wallpaper, pee on your favorite rug, or get into the trash. That means you won't come home and get

mad at him for doing what puppies do: explore, destroy, chew, and eliminate. Some people even place a dog crate or puppy playpen in several different rooms, such as the living room, bedroom, and home office, so that the puppy always has a safe place to be when he's not being watched.

Your job is to reduce your puppy's chances of making a mistake, and a crate is a good way to accomplish that. Using a crate is much kinder than banishing a dog to the basement, garage, or backyard so that he never learns how to be responsible in the house, and the cost of a crate is much less than the cost of repairing chewed-up woodwork or furniture.

A crate should be just large enough for your dog to stand up, turn around, and stretch out on his side. If the crate is too big, your pup will be able to eliminate at one end of the crate and sleep at the other. If your little puppy is going to grow into a large adult, buy a crate suited to his adult size, but block off part of it with a box or divider. As your pup grows, you can increase the amount of space he has in the crate until a divider is no longer needed.

To teach your puppy that the crate is a happy place, give him a treat each time he goes inside. As he steps inside, say, "Crate!" or "Bed!" in a happy tone of voice. It's always a good idea to assign a name to each action you want your puppy to learn. Soon, he'll go racing to his crate whenever you say the magic word. Be sure to reward him with praise and a treat, and leave a safe chew toy inside for him to play with. Place the crate in a

busy area of the house such as the den or kitchen so he doesn't feel abandoned when he's in it. You can feed your puppy meals in the crate, which is also a good way to increase your pup's positive association with the crate.

Keep in mind that crates can be misused. Your pup should not be confined to his crate for more than three or four hours at a time during the day. It is cruel to leave a young pup in a crate all day long when no one is at home. It's counterproductive and leaves your puppy no choice but to eliminate in his crate, which defeats the crate's role in

house-training. The crate is meant to be your pup's den area, and if he learns to soil the crate, it will be even more difficult to house-train him. (Be aware that crate-training often does not work with puppies from pet stores because they have learned that eliminating in a cage is normal.) If you have to leave your pup for an extended period of time, put the open crate in a safe room as described above.

It's important, too, that the crate not be used as a place of punishment. Never crate your puppy in anger. His crate should always be a safe haven he can go to for a nap or to get away from the tugging fingers of toddlers. Be sure your children know that the crate is Duke's special room, where he's not to be bothered.

At night, let your pup sleep in his crate next to your bed. He'll be comforted by your presence, and in the morning, you'll be aware of any restlessness indicating he's ready to go out. It's important to avoid teaching your puppy that whining or barking will get him released from the

crate. Wait until he's quiet before opening the door. He should be able to go the entire night without an accident, especially if he's more than three months old. (If your pup does need to go out in the middle of the night, put him right back in his crate after he has performed so he learns that nighttime isn't playtime.)

Preventing Potty Problems

Watching your puppy when he's outside his safe place is crucial. If you don't watch him, you won't be able to prevent accidents. A good way to keep your puppy from wandering off and having an accident while your back is turned is to leash him and keep him at your side. He'll enjoy being with you, and you'll notice immediately if he needs to go out. Give him a toy to play with while he's next to you. If you're doing something that doesn't allow you to keep a close watch on your puppy, put him in his crate, playpen, or safe room. This will help prevent any accidents.

Every time you notice your puppy sniffing, circling, or squatting, clap your hands to get his attention and, say, "Outside? Do you need to go outside?" Then hustle him out before he has a chance to do anything. Set a timer so that you remember to take him out every hour or two, even if he doesn't show any signs of needing to go out. Always take your pup out on a leash so you can see him potty, and praise him when he does. Giving a small food reward, such as a bit of kibble, immediately after your pup potties further reinforces the habit of eliminating outdoors. Consistent positive reinforcement is the key to successful house-training.

It's very important that you go outside with your puppy. If you aren't there with him, you can't praise him for eliminating or teach him the go potty command. You also have no way of knowing whether he actually did anything. Many pet own-

ers get angry because they send their pup outside and then the pup pees or poops when he comes inside. Without your guidance, your pup doesn't know why he's outside. If he hasn't performed after fifteen or twenty minutes, take him inside and crate him. Try again later.

What Goes in Must Come Out

Another way to help your puppy potty on schedule is to feed him at set times each day rather than leaving food out and allowing him to nibble all day long. When your dog eats at the same times every day, it's easier to gauge when he'll need to go out. Feed your young pup after his first elimination of the day, once in midafternoon, and again in the evening, spacing his meals about six hours apart. Feeding your pup high-quality, highly digestible food helps keep him on schedule as well. The ingredients in these foods produce less stool volume, meaning your puppy won't have to eliminate as often.

Eating stimulates your pup's bowels, so take him outside after every meal. Give him a couple of minutes to do his business and if he doesn't potty, take him back inside and crate him so that he doesn't potty in the house. Try again in ten minutes. Keep taking him out at ten-minute intervals until he performs, paying attention to the amount of time that elapses between the end of the meal and when he finally potties. Most pups need to go thirty to sixty minutes after eating. If you know your pup's needs, you can keep him on schedule and avoid accidents.

Accidents Happen

Your puppy is bound to make mistakes, especially in the first few weeks of house-training. Always remember that he is just a baby—no matter what his size—and that he needs time to learn. You are his teacher, and he relies on you to make sure that he gets plenty of opportunities to do things right.

If your pup pees or poops in the house, don't yell at him. Instead, make a note to yourself to watch him more closely and take him out more frequently. Then gently put him in his crate or the safe room, and clean up the mess. Remember: reward correct behavior and ignore unwanted behavior. Never rub his nose in the mess or swat him with a rolled-up newspaper, or anything else. Not only will anger and punishment increase stress and fear in your puppy, but he'll also become sneaky about finding places to potty.

If you catch your puppy in the act of eliminating in the house, clap your hands to get his attention and, say, "Aaaaght Outside." If he stops (unlikely), take him outside to finish. Avoid saying "No" or

HONEY, ACTUALLY, SHE IS STILL A PUPPY.

calling him a bad dog. You don't want him to think that the act of eliminating is wrong, you just want him to know that he chose the wrong place.

Until your pup is reliable, don't let him run free in your home. A puppy who is eliminating everywhere in the house has too much freedom. Instead, keep him by your side or confined to his safe room or crate. This is especially important during busy times of the day such as mornings and dinnertime, when you have less time to watch him. It is important to restrict his access to certain areas within the house until he starts eliminating outdoors on a regular basis.

Part of house-training is being able to read your pup's cues. Dogs have different ways of letting you know when they need to go out. Some dogs bark or run to the door, but others are subtle in their communications, which they limit to staring or twitching their ears a certain way. Many dogs learn to ring a bell when they want to go out. To teach this trick, hang a bell on the doorknob or on the wall next to the door. Be sure it's within your pup's reach. Every time you take him out for a potty run, ring the bell before you go out the door. When he

rings the bell on his own, praise him and take him out. Whatever the sound or behavior, watch your pup closely to learn his signals.

If you're having problems house-training your puppy, make sure you're being consistent with your training methods. Don't try method after method, quickly switching from one to another. Choose the method you want to use, and stick with it. Otherwise, your pup will become confused. Keep in mind, too, that house-training accidents—especially after a pup seems reliable—may indicate a health problem. Take your puppy to a veterinarian for an exam if he suddenly breaks house-training for no apparent reason. He may have a bladder or kidney infection.

Cleaning Up

There's a technique to removing stains and odors caused by puppy waste. If done properly, your carpet can look and smell as good as new.

When you're dealing with urine, the first step is to sop up as much of the liquid as possible. Keep a supply of ratty old towels on hand for this job. When you've absorbed as much moisture as possible, saturate the spot with the cleanser of your choice. Many pet owners find success using products such as Resolve, OdorMute, Nature's Miracle, Simple Solution, and Anti-Icky-Poo. Others simply use white vinegar. Avoid using ammonia or any cleansers that contain ammonia; ammonia is a component of urine, and its scent will draw your pup back to that spot again and again.

Once you've applied the cleanser, use a clean towel or rag to blot the area again. Then get a dry towel, place it over the area, and pile some heavy books on top of it. No, your puppy won't read them while he's on the toilet, but the weight of the books presses the towel into the carpet drawing out more moisture. Leave the books on the spot overnight or until the area is dry. Sprinkle the spot with baking powder to help wick away moisture and vacuum it up when the spot is dry.

You can soak up moisture with a wet vacuum, too.

If you can smell that your pup has had an accident but can't find the spot, use a black light to find the stain on the carpet. Saturate the area with your chosen cleanser and follow the steps described above.

For solid waste, use a towel or rag to pick up as much of the mess as possible. Dump the stool in the toilet, and toss the towel in a bucket for a hot-water wash later on. Just as parents keep diaper pails, many pet owners keep a bucket handy to hold all the towels and rags used to clean up urine, stool, and vomit.

When you've removed as much waste as you can, apply your chosen cleanser and use another rag to get up any remaining bits. Enzyme-based cleansers that digest waste such as OdorMute are especially good for this purpose. Then get a clean towel and use a wet vacuum or the book technique described

above until the spot is dry. Until your pup is fully house-trained, it's a good idea to have your carpet professionally cleaned periodically.

Most important, be patient. Taking the time to train your puppy properly early in his life will pay off many times through the years.

Chewing

Why Do Dogs Chew?

They gnaw on knickknacks, suck on socks, chew on chair legs. Their destructive power is roughly equivalent to that of a minor atomic weapon—at least, that's the way it looks when you discover it. Stuffing pulled out of sofas, new designs nibbled into wallpaper, drywall exposed, wood floors destroyed. All this, while brand-new chew toys lie in the rubble, still pristine.

What causes dogs to chew and chew and chew? And how can you channel their chewing constructively?

Dogs chew for many reasons. Young dogs have a physiological need to chew. Chewing helps them to exercise and develop their jaws. Six-week-old puppies have a set of baby teeth (your veterinarian may refer to them as deciduous teeth). Through the process of teething, all the baby teeth will eventually be replaced by permanent teeth. Puppies start to lose their baby teeth when they're six to seven months old, but permanent

teeth don't fully come in until dogs are about one year old. During this time, puppies chew a lot. Chewing helps relieve the pain of teething and is a perfectly normal part of puppy growth and development. One solution to help relieve teething pain is to freeze an old wet washcloth and give it to your pup to chew on.

Puppies also go through an intense play period, and one of the things that puppies do in play is chew. It's fun to chew things up and see the pieces go flying!

Older dogs chew because it's pleasurable or sooth-ing for them. Chewing helps relieve boredom. It also helps keep dogs' teeth and gums strong and healthy. Dogs with irritated or painful gums from gingivitis may chew excessively to help relieve the pain. Some dogs chew when they're feeling nervous or stressed. Often, their chewing results from separation anxiety. In all these instances, chewing is a repetitive activity

that's soothing and just plain feels good. Sort of like playing solitaire.

Of all the reasons dogs chew, spite isn't one of them. You may feel as if your dog has destroyed your favorite pair of $200 sandals because you don't spend enough time with her, but face it, dogs just aren't wired that way. While they're pretty darn smart, they aren't capable of thinking, *I'll teach her to leave me alone for twelve hours straight. I'll go find her favorite, most expensive pair of shoes and eat them!* The belief that dogs do things to get back at us is a myth that should have been retired long ago.

Now that you know why dogs chew, it's time to examine your dog's chewing habits and your responses to them. Believe it or not, your dog can learn to chew just her toys, not yours. Teaching your dog what's okay to chew and what's not takes patience and consistency, but the savings in money and frustration are well worth the effort. And when your puppy is chewing on a toy, she's not barking, digging, or otherwise getting into trouble.

When Chewing Becomes a Problem

We often think that puppy chewing is cute. We might say, "Look at her toss her head with that envelope in her mouth!" We ignore this cute behavior until something valuable is destroyed, then we want to put a stop to it. By that time,

however, the chewing of anything and everything is a habit that's difficult to break.

Preventing inappropriate chewing is not just good for your furniture and clothing but can save your dog's life. Dogs who chew electrical cords run the risk of death by electrocution. Dogs who steal garbage, cat food, or rich treats are at risk for pancreatitis, a potentially fatal inflammation of the pancreas. Dogs who eat socks, rocks, or children's toys can suffer life-threatening intestinal blockages.

Destructive chewing is also harmful to your dog, as it frequently causes feelings of boredom, loneliness, and isolation. Dogs are intelligent, social animals who need the stimulation of activity and companionship. The psychological stress of being left alone on a regular basis can lead to phobias or anxieties that result in chewing as escape behavior (for instance, chewing through doors or windows) or chewing for relief (for example, when the dog is left alone or when a change occurs in the household, such as a new baby or a new work schedule).

Because chewing is so enjoyable and calming, dogs want to do it again and again. That desire to

chew can become a good habit or a bad habit, depending on what dogs learn to chew and the quality of interaction they have with their owners.

If you have a puppy, you'll need to start teaching her good habits in puppyhood. Given the opportunity, she's going to chew everything she can get her teeth on. Besides being entertaining,

it's simply her way of exploring her territory. When your puppy decides to chew on an electrical cord, it's because she doesn't yet know that the cord isn't a toy like her hard rubber ball or bone. Teaching your puppy right chewing from wrong chewing requires a two-pronged approach: making your home safe for the puppy (and from the puppy) and redirecting improper chewing.

Dog-Proofing Your Home

Just like infants, puppies put anything and everything in their mouths. One veterinarian says he is astounded by the variety of things puppies will chew on or swallow. With that in mind, it's a priority for new puppy owners or owners of chewers to take steps to remove temptations or make them unappealing or inaccessible. (The bonus to this is usually a neater, less-cluttered home.)

Smell is often what first attracts a dog to a forbidden item. Things that smell good to a dog range from stinky socks to leather shoes to ripe garbage. Make it a habit to put laundry in hampers, shoes in closed closets, and trash containers inside cabinets. If there's no room for the trash beneath the kitchen or bathroom sink, buy containers with locking lids. Avoid small decorative trash cans, which are just the right size for an inquisitive puppy to stick his nose into and pull out such shreddable treasures as envelopes and used tissues. Put small trash cans on top of your dresser or bathroom counter.

Secure heavy items that could fall on your puppy. Remind family members to pick up toys, clothes, remote controls, eyeglasses, and briefcases. Take up throw rugs, and put plants out of reach. Don't leave the ends of toilet paper hanging down. Everything is fodder for the puppy chewing machine.

Dog-proofing your home is more than just keeping things picked up. You need to look at things

from a dog's eye view. In each room, get down on your hands and knees so you can see what your pup sees. Doesn't the carving on that table leg look interesting? And look at all those cords underneath the desk where the kids do their homework.

Tape down cords for lamps and electronic equipment. Wrap the cords and bind them with plastic cable ties, (available at electronics stores), or coat them with Bitter Apple or another unappetizing substance, such as hot sauce or a solution of cayenne pepper mixed with water. You can also try covering cords in aluminum foil. Many dogs don't enjoy biting down on the silvery wrap. Avoid wrapping frayed cords with aluminum foil, as it could serve as a conductor for electricity. If cords are frayed, it's best to replace them anyway. They aren't safe, even without a puppy around.

If your puppy shows interest in chewing on walls or furniture legs, coat the attractive area with a nasty-tasting substance, such as Bitter Apple, citronella oil, or hot sauce. (Apply it first in an inconspicuous area to make sure it doesn't harm the finish.) Not every dog finds these concoctions unpleasant; some even seem to think they just add to the flavor. They're worth a try, however.

Forget the idea of giving your puppy old socks or shoes to chew on. She can't tell the difference between those and your good shoes and socks, so don't run the risk of confusing her.

If there's a room in your home that's not safe for a curious dog, keep it off limits with a baby gate

or other barrier. Be sure the pup can't stick her head through the gate and get stuck. If baby gates don't work for your situation, close doors or keep the puppy leashed at your side.

Find one room in your home that can be a place where your puppy can go freely. This is usually a kitchen, laundry room, or bathroom. Be sure to stock this room with several approved toys. Even in a "safe" room, however, your pup may take it into her head to nibble on the baseboards, cabinets, or wall. For repairs, keep cans of paint and spackling handy but out of reach.

The most important step in avoiding chewing disasters is, well, preventing them. When you can't be around to supervise, confine your dog to the safe room or to a crate, along with a toy to keep her occupied. That way, she can't get into trouble, and you won't get mad at her.

When a crate is introduced and used correctly, it's a kind, effective way to keep a puppy or dog out of harm's way. Help the puppy feel at home in her crate by feeding her in it, and never use crate

time as a means of punishment. If you take these steps, your dog will feel safe in her cozy den—which should be just large enough for her to lie down, stand up, and turn around in—and your belongings will be protected from the depredations of sharp puppy teeth.

If your dog is younger than six months old, don't confine her to a crate or safe room for more than four hours at a time without giving her an opportunity to take a potty break. Dogs this young simply aren't capable of "holding it" for much longer than that.

What Should Dogs Chew?

Your dog needs a variety of chew toys. She should have at least half a dozen—many trainers recommend more—of different sizes, shapes, and textures. Which toy your dog prefers may depend on her mood or what game she wants to play.

Rotate toys weekly so that only a few are out at any one time. This helps prevent boredom. When you bring out the other toys, they'll seem like new. Place the current week's toys in a toy box or other container your dog can easily access so she can choose what she wants to play with.

Toys for dogs range from the classic rawhides and hard rubber bones to stuffed cuddle toys to interactive items, such as Action Balls or Buster Cubes, which can be filled with bite-sized treats. Whatever you choose should be both practical and long lasting, able to withstand a lot of high-energy play. The best chew toys are safe, fun, easy to clean, inedible, and hard-wearing items that are different from your own belongings.

Avoid toys that resemble or are made from household items you wouldn't want destroyed. This includes toy shoes or tugs made from old socks. It's less expensive to buy dog toys than it is to replace good clothes or shoes that are mistaken for toys. If your child has a favorite teddy bear or other stuffed animal, be sure it's kept separate from the dog's stuffed animals.

Beware of other toys that contain small hard parts or bells, buttons, and squeakers that could be swallowed. Rawhide bones are controversial because many dogs gobble them down and can choke or suffer digestive blockages when large

pieces are swallowed. Most trainers recommend giving rawhide only under supervision and removing the bone when the dog is left alone. If you choose to give rawhide, look for compressed rawhide, which is less likely to break down in the intestinal tract.

Favorite dog toys are Kongs, Nylabones, Buster Cubes, tennis balls, rope toys, Cressite or other solid-rubber balls, Star Balls, Mutt Pucks, and soft objects, such as stuffed animals or fleece toys, especially those that make squeaky sounds.

Kongs and Star Balls bounce erratically, so they're interesting for dogs to chase. Tennis balls are beloved by retrievers everywhere. The fibers of rope and sheepskin toys help keep a dog's teeth clean, similar to what flossing does for humans. Handle soft toys frequently so they hold your scent. Your dog will love snuggling with them when you're not home. This is especially important for dogs with separation anxiety.

Buster Cubes, Goodie Grippers, Kongs, and similar toys are great for keeping dogs occupied for long periods because they can be stuffed with treats, such as peanut butter, soft cheese spreads, raw baby carrots, kibble, and biscuits, so that dogs have to work to get them out. You can make rubber toys, such as Nylabones or Mutt Pucks, more appealing to your dog by coating them with bacon grease, peanut butter, or cheese. (Remember to clean and disinfect all these toys on a regular basis. Most can be run through the dishwasher.)

Special chew treats can be made by stuffing a hollowed, sterilized beef marrow bone with a thick filling of kibble mixed with water. Mix equal amounts of kibble and water and let the mixture sit for an hour to soften. Fill the bone and freeze it overnight, then "frost" the ends with a soft cheese or peanut butter. This is likely to make a mess as it's chewed, so give it outdoors and under supervision to make sure your dog doesn't swallow any bone fragments.

Even the best toys have a finite life span. Replace toys with broken or sharp edges, loose squeakers, or small, easily swallowed parts. Get rid of rawhide toys that have softened or come apart, as well as rope toys that don't have knotted ends. Sew up or discard soft toys that are coming unstuffed. If your dog has a special favorite, keep a couple of extras of that type of toy so that a replacement is available when the old one bites the dust.

Teaching Your Dog to Chew Toys

Too often we assume that a dog instinctively knows that her toys are there for her to chew, and she may play with them for a time. But she needs to be taught that she is permitted to chew only those toys and not any other household items. This is easy to do using positive reinforcement.

Any time you see your dog chewing on her dog toy, tell her what a good dog she is. To further reinforce her good behavior, try clicker training. Get a

clicker at a pet supply store or toy store. When you notice her chewing on her toy, click once, then immediately give her a treat and praise her.

Play games such as fetch with your puppy's toys so she associates them with good times. Keep toys in every room so your dog always has something good to chew on. Remember to handle toys frequently so they have your scent. You can make them more appealing by stuffing them with treats or peanut butter.

Give each toy a name, such as "red ball" or "rope bone." Dogs can understand large vocabularies, and many are capable of distinguishing between, say, their green frog and their red ball, their bone and their Kong.

When your dog brings you a toy, praise her. Then start putting a name to the action: "Good get your toy!" Start telling her to get her toy and reward her when she complies. Click, treat, and praise if you're using clicker training.

Another fun game is to scatter toys throughout the house. Walk to each room with your dog, and

tell her to find her toy. When she picks up the toy, reward her with praise and a treat, or click and a treat.

Teach your dog to greet you with a toy in her mouth. When you come home tell her to find her toy. Withhold petting or other attention until she's clutching a toy. When she knows it's about time for you to get home, she'll start looking for a toy to chew on in preparation for your arrival.

To test your dog's knowledge of what she should and shouldn't chew, set out several chew toys, plus a forbidden item, such as a paperback book or a plastic yogurt container. Have a noise-maker handy, such as an empty soda can with a few pennies inside. (Tape the lid so the coins don't fall out.) Ask her to get her toy and reward her with praise and a treat if she chooses an appropriate item.

If she picks up something other than a toy, clap your hands, then say, "Aaaack, drop it!" or other-

wise startle her into letting go of the item. It may be useful to have a helper who can toss the shake can in the pup's direction (don't hit her with it!) if she picks up the wrong thing. Then repeat the command to get a toy, and reward her when she chooses correctly. With practice, you should eventually be able to present her with many inappropriate items and only one toy and have her always choose the toy.

Some puppies run away with the item they're chewing. Don't chase after her. Instead, run in the opposite direction, encouraging your dog to chase after you. If she drops the item when she runs after you, that's good. Give her a toy and praise her. If she doesn't drop it, calmly take the item away when she gets to you and replace it with a toy.

Any kind of positive reinforcement works much better than punishment when it comes to teaching puppies right from wrong. But there will always be instances when your puppy or dog backslides or tries to chew on something dangerous. In the following section you can learn several ways you can change your dog's behavior and set her jaws back on the right path.

Ways to Redirect Problem Chewing

If you catch your dog chewing on something forbidden, distract her by tossing a shake can or other noisemaker in her direction. The sound should startle the puppy into dropping or leaving the unacceptable item. Then give her a toy, and click, treat, and praise when she chews on or plays with the toy.

Correction is especially important when your pup is trying to chew something dangerous, such as an electrical cord. You can't afford to let her learn a shocking lesson on her own, so you need to correct the behavior instantly, making it so unpleasant that the dog won't even want to try chewing cords again.

To put a stop to this type of inappropriate chewing, give the dog an immediate verbal warning that what she's doing is wrong. Call out, "Aaaack!" or "No!" Within two to five seconds—the sooner the better—follow the verbal warning with a physical correction, such as squirting the dog with water from a spray bottle or tossing a throw pillow in her direction (don't hit her with it). Once she's distracted from bad chewing, give her a toy or tell her to go get a toy, then praise her for chewing the toy. Then try to find a way to make

the dangerous item inaccessible or unpleasant.

For dogs who are trash hounds, try booby-trapping the garbage. Place pot lids or empty aluminum cans on top of the garbage can. When your dog tries to get into the trash, the lids or cans will clatter down, startling her with their noise.

If you come home and find something chewed up, there's no point in yelling at your dog about it. She won't understand what she did wrong.

Correct her only when you catch her in the act of chewing the wrong thing. Just as important, if not more so, praise her when you catch her chewing the right thing. Remember, as well, that too much punishment and not enough training and praise will simply teach your dog to do her destructive chewing in secret.

You can also prevent destructive chewing by confining the dog when you can't be there to supervise. Crating her or putting her in a dog-proofed room protects your belongings and pro-tects your dog from a scolding that she won't understand. Be sure you give her a safe chew toy that is stuffed with goodies, so she'll have some-thing to occupy her while you're gone. This is especially important for dogs younger than two years of age. Even though they look full grown, they're still puppies emotionally and physically and should not be given free run of the house until they've proven themselves trustworthy.

One of the best ways to avert destructive chew-ing is to give your dog plenty of exercise. To paraphrase an old saying, idle paws are the devil's workshop. Just like children, dogs need a lot of play to keep them physically and mentally fit. Highly active dogs, such as Labrador retrievers or Jack Russell terriers, need as much as one to two hours of exercise daily. When they don't get enough activity, they turn their clever canine minds to finding

their own entertainment, and their choice of entertainment frequently involves chewing.

Take your dog for a half-hour walk in the morning before you leave for work. The exercise will help her relax, making her less likely to chew destructively. Include some training practice, such as sitting or heeling, while you walk to give her some mental stimulation. On a rainy day or when you're running short of time, play fetch in the house for fifteen or twenty minutes. Toss a ball down the hall or stairs for your dog to retrieve. Another walk or play session in the evening will help your dog settle down for bedtime.

If your dog is chewing excessively or destructively and hasn't responded to training and redirection, take her to the veterinarian to rule out an underlying medical cause, such as a nutritional deficiency. Your veterinarian can also help you figure out if the chewing is related to a phobia or to separation anxiety, or the doctor may refer you to a behaviorist who can help.

Preventing a Chewing Problem

If you have a puppy, spend the time now to keep her need to chew from becoming a chewing problem. To help prevent separation anxiety and related chewing, gradually introduce your dog to the concept of being left alone. Start by leaving her for only five or ten minutes at a time. You need to teach your dog that you will always come back.

Slowly increase the amount of time you're gone, and be sure your dog has toys to keep her occupied. If she has a couple of favorite toys,

consider making them even more special by giving them to her only at times when you'll be gone. It can also help to leave the radio or television on so she'll have the comfort of human voices.

When you leave the house, do it matter-of-factly, and when you return, ignore the dog for the first few minutes after arrival. Making a big production out of leaving or arriving gives the dog the idea that being alone is bad and your return is exciting. Instead, you want her to view arrivals and departures as routine. Fun things, such as going for a walk or being fed, should be postponed until you've been home for a little while.

It's also important to teach your dog early on that she can't get attention any time she wants it. If you are busy and your dog is bugging you for attention, it's okay to put her in her crate for a nap while you finish what you need to do. Instead of petting her or playing with her every time she asks, first require her to perform a command, such as *sit* or *down*. This technique is called "learn to earn" and establishes your leadership.

If your dog is younger than two years of age, consider crating her or leaving her in a safe room or a dog run whenever you can't be there to supervise. Dogs this young are rarely capable of being reliable in the house. It's your responsibility to keep them from getting into trouble. A dog who always receives a scolding when her owner returns home will simply become more and more anxious every time she's left alone. A dog who's confined, however, is unable to get into trouble and, thus, is less prone to anxiety.

Whatever the cause, chewing is not a behavior that your dog will magically outgrow. She needs your guidance to learn what to chew, and spending time with you is the only way she can learn your rules.

Digging

Why Do Dogs Dig?

Are they digging to China? Looking for buried treasure? Conducting an archaeological excavation? Preparing a foundation for a new doghouse? As obsessively as some dogs dig, it certainly seems as if they must have some higher purpose for digging.

Digging is a perfectly normal behavior for dogs. Your rottweiler, Scottie, or husky isn't digging to make you angry, he's just doing what comes

naturally. Some dogs are born to dig, especially the terriers, who were bred to seek out underground prey such as moles, foxes, and badgers, and the Nordic breeds, whose ancestors dug snow caves to keep warm in the frozen wastes of their homeland. Digging is a remnant of the survival skills needed by ancient dogs. Before dogs became domesticated, they dug to store or find food and to create shelter for themselves and their pups. When you see your dog dig, you're watching heredity in action.

When not given other activities to occupy their minds, terriers and herding, working, or sporting dogs will dig. After all, these are dogs who were bred to have a mission, whether that was to go on

rodent search-and-destroy missions, seek out and retrieve game, pull sleds or carts, herd livestock, or stand guard. They need to have a job, and if they aren't given one, well, digging will have to do.

Some dogs dig simply to mimic their owners whom they see "playing" in the dirt while gardening or doing yard work. Digging is good exercise too. It's a great workout for a dog's upper body and legs. We do aerobics, dogs dig.

Among the reasons dogs dig, entertainment, prey, shelter, attention, anxiety, and escape are the more popular. But there is a reason that dogs *don't* dig, and that's for spite. We often think that dogs dig up the yard out of revenge because we don't spend enough time with them, but, dogs just aren't programmed that way. While they're pretty darn smart, they aren't capable of thinking, *I'll teach her to leave me alone for twelve hours straight. I'll dig a hole the size of a swimming pool!* The belief that dogs do things to get back at us is a myth that should have long since been retired.

Just because digging is normal, however, doesn't always make it acceptable. Excessive or inappropriate digging can damage or destroy yards, gardens, carpets, and walls. A dog who escapes the yard by digging is exposed to such hazards as being hit by a car, or attacked by another dog, not to mention the possibilities of unwanted pregnancies or contagious diseases.

How can you stop, or at least channel, digging so that it's less destructive? Study the reasons for digging on the following pages and ask yourself whether any of them apply to your dog. Once you've determined why your dog behaves the way he does, you can use the suggestions in this book to solve your digging problem.

Digging for Fun

Digging is a lot of fun for dogs. If you think about it, a dog's digging behavior is similar to a child's enjoyment of making mud pies or finger painting. Dirt smells good when it's dug up, and tree roots can take the place of a tug toy, with the tree holding the other end of the "toy."

Dogs often dig for entertainment when they spend a lot of time alone in a yard, especially if they're left without toys. Puppies and young dogs up to three years of age dig for fun when they don't have other outlets for their energy.

If your dog digs for fun, you can often redirect his energy by spending more time with him, giving him more exercise, and providing him with interesting toys. A half-hour walk once or twice a day helps your dog expend excess energy, plus it's good exercise for you too!

Puppies need even more exercise. Take yours for on-leash walks at least four times a day (after meals and naps) and provide a couple of playtime ses-

sions in your backyard if it's fenced so he can run off leash. Remember, just because your dog has a big yard doesn't mean he will exercise himself. Just like us, dogs need motivation, and in most cases that motivation is the presence of their people.

Dogs enjoy playing with their owners. Take some time every day to play with your dog by tossing a ball or flying disc, playing tug, or practicing tricks or agility routines. Take an obedience class with your dog and practice the commands you learn every day, but practice for only a few minutes at a stretch. You want your dog tired, not wired.

When you can't be there to play with your dog, make sure he has several interesting toys to keep him occupied. Good choices include Kongs or Giggle Balls that are stuffed with treats, and balls of different sizes that can be rolled around the yard. Tennis balls, soccer balls, and basketballs are good choices, depending on the type of dog you have. Rotate toys so your dog always has something different to play with.

If you feed dry kibble, make your dog work for his meals. In the morning, before you leave for work, fill a Buster Cube or similar toy with the amount of food your dog gets for breakfast. The hole releases the food as the dog rolls the toy. This is your dog's big chance to hunt for his food instead of having it handed to him in a silver doggy dish. The activity will keep him too busy to dig.

Provide an area where it's okay to dig and teach your dog to use it. A remote area of the yard, or any place you don't mind a few holes, is a good start. Decide on an area and allot about four square feet. Shady areas are good choices as they help your dog stay cool. A child's sandbox or a plastic wading pool are also good alternatives. Some people prefer sand because it doesn't turn into mud when it gets wet, and it's easy for the dog to shake off.

When you have decided on a digging area, cover it with about two feet of sand or loose soil. You can define or disguise the area by surrounding it with rocks, shrubs, two-by-fours, railroad ties, or even a low decorative fence. (Keep in mind that sandy, shady areas can attract fleas.

Keep them at bay by mixing small amounts of diatomaceous earth (DE) in with the sand. Be careful not to breathe in the DE dust.)

Let your dog see you bury some toys or treats in the area. Encourage him to dig them up, and praise him when he does. Keep seeding the area with interesting items so that he wants to return to it. If you catch your dog digging in a forbidden area, say, "No dig" and take him to his digging pit. Say, "Dig" in a happy tone of voice, and praise him when he does, saying, "Good dig." Providing a special digging area works best for dogs who dig for fun, not for those who dig in search of prey or to find an escape route.

If your dog just flat out prefers a hole in the ground, set up an approved digging area as described above, or learn to live with one or two holes in your yard. Taking a dog's hole away is like throwing out your spouse's favorite recliner or your comfortable mattress.

Digging for Prey

When dogs dig to pursue prey, they're just following their instincts. Their acute hearing and excellent sense of smell make them aware of underground critters such as gophers, snakes, and bugs that we're completely unaware of. Other odors dogs might smell underground are dead animals or long-buried trash. Some signs that indicate that your dog is seeking out burrowing animals, insects, or other buried treasure include a hole in a specific area (rather than at the boundary of the yard), a hole at the roots of a tree or shrub, or a trench.

Dogs who dig for prey can be more difficult to deal with because they're likely to have a never-

ending supply of varmints, and they're so proud when they present you with their prize. But there are steps you can take to try to rid your yard of moles and other critters.

If your dog is hunting moles or gophers, get rid of the grubs in your yard—they're a mole's favorite food. Ask a garden shop for advice on getting rid of these varmints. Avoid using poison to get at moles or insects; it could end up killing your dog instead of the pests.

When pest extermination isn't an option, consider confining your dog to a secure run or an area

of the yard that has a concrete, wood, or brick surface. Give him plenty of toys to keep him occupied and perhaps a sandbox that he can dig in. Cover the ground inside the run with gravel, tiles, or concrete so your dog can't dig his way out. Don't forget to exercise him before he goes in the run and after he gets out.

Digging for Shelter

Dogs are den animals, and many dogs dig to provide themselves with shelter. Evidence of a shelter-digging dog is a hole the length and width of the dog's body.

Dogs usually dig near the foundation of buildings, large shade trees, or water sources. They may dig several holes around the yard so that they always have a shady place to lie as the sun moves. In hot weather, dogs dig to lie in the cool dirt, and in cold weather they may dig to build a barrier against wind. A dog who digs for this reason often

lacks a doghouse or has a doghouse that's placed in an area that's too hot or windy. Other dogs prefer to be closer to their owners, so they dig a sleeping hole that's as close to the house as possible such as under the porch.

To remedy shelter digging, provide other options to your dog for staying cool. Move the doghouse to a shady area or purchase an insulated doghouse, set up a large umbrella in the yard, or provide a child's wading pool filled with cool water. This is a great idea for water-loving dogs such as Labrador retrievers and Newfoundlands. If the weather gets really hot, let your dog stay indoors or in a cool basement. Be sure fresh drinking water is always available. In winter, provide the doghouse with warm, clean bedding and change it regularly.

Digging for Attention

Dogs who are frequently left alone dig to get attention. After all, any attention—even if it involves being yelled at—is better than none. Consider this possibility if your dog digs only when you're around or if he doesn't get much of a chance to spend time with the family.

The remedy: spend more time with your dog in the house—your dog wants to be with you. Spending ten minutes in the morning and evening with him is not enough. Your dog would much rather keep you company than dig holes by himself, even if all you're doing is watching television or puttering around the house. Dogs who feel as if they're part of the family are less likely to have behavior problems.

This means that it's important for your dog to have good house manners so you'll want him to be around. Train your dog to have manners by taking him to obedience class and practicing the commands on a regular basis. Training helps

establish trust, respect, and control, and like any-thing else, requires regular practice and reinforce-ment if it's to be retained.

Besides the basic commands *sit, down, stay,* and *come,* ask the trainer to help you teach *leave it.* This command comes in handy when you want your dog to stop digging and come to you. It doesn't hurt to take a class every year or two, just to provide socialization and learn new things.

Consider getting a second dog to keep your dog company. The advantage of a second dog is that the two can spend hours playing with each other. The potential disadvantage is that two dogs can dig more holes than a single dog. If you decide to get a second dog, you will still need to provide toys and regular out-of-yard exercise. Also, if your first dog is a breed who is wired to dig, try to choose a second dog with a nondig-ging heritage.

If getting a second dog isn't an option, consider signing up your pet for doggy day care. Many boarding kennels and veterinary offices provide

this service. Day care gives your dog the opportunity to interact with other dogs and people during the day and may even provide training practice or games, such as agility and flyball, which will wear your dog out. Not every city has doggy day care facilities, but you may be able to trade off with a neighbor or friend, or pay a local teenager to play with your dog after school.

Digging out of Anxiety

Since dogs are intelligent, social animals who need the stimulation of activity and companionship, boredom, loneliness, and isolation frequently cause destructive digging. Digging is a repetitive activity that can be comforting and help relieve anxiety, stress, or nervousness. It may even be an attempt to find the missing family. This kind of digging isn't limited to outdoor dogs; dogs left alone indoors have been known to dig into carpet or through doors or walls in an attempt to find their owners.

To help prevent separation anxiety, gradually introduce your dog to the concept of being left

alone. Start by leaving him for five or ten minutes at a time. He needs to learn that you will always come back. Slowly increase the amount of time you're gone, and be sure your dog has toys to keep him occupied. If he has a couple of favorite toys, consider making them even more special by giving them to him only when you're gone.

When you leave, do it matter-of-factly, and ignore your dog for the first few minutes upon your return. Making a big production out of leaving or arriving gives a dog the idea that being alone is bad and puts too much importance and excitement on your return. Instead, you want your dog to view arrivals and departures as routine. Fun activities such as going for a walk or being fed should be postponed until you've been home for a little while.

In extreme cases, ask your veterinarian or a qualified behaviorist for help. Behavior modification training and, if necessary, medications can be prescribed to help keep your dog calm until behavior modification techniques can work.

Digging to Escape

The psychological stress of being left alone on a regular basis can lead to phobias or anxiety that result in digging as escape behavior, such as digging through doors or escaping a boring situation by digging beneath the fence to see what or who is on the other side. Scent hounds such as beagles, bloodhounds, and coonhounds are likely to

dig and escape because they want to follow any scent they catch in the air, and no puny fence is going to stop them.

Dogs who aren't altered tend to have an abundance of sexual energy and usually dig along the fence line or under the fence to escape and find a mate. Intact males and females will climb every mountain and cross every sea in an attempt to find a sexual companion. Sexual tension can be lessened with the introduction of another altered dog. To alleviate this type of digging problem, spay or neuter your dog. Along with health benefits, altered dogs are more affectionate toward their owners and less likely to wander off.

Exploration is another common canine activity that causes digging as escape behavior. Dogs explore to find food and perhaps to expand their territory. If your dog escapes to go exploring, take him on regular walks to different places to satisfy his curiosity.

More Ways to Prevent Digging

Prevent access to your dog's favorite digging areas. If he likes to dig in your garden because the turned soil has an attractive scent, fence off the area with a decorative picket fence or confine him to a run when you can't be around to supervise. It's believed that some dogs dig in gardens because they see their owners digging there. It can't hurt to put your dog in the house while you're planting your garden—just to keep him from getting any ideas.

Some dogs bury bones or other food items and later dig them up for consumption. Try putting a halt to this by feeding your dog indoors and only at specific times. He should get enough food for his needs but not so much that he has enough to hide for later. Pick up his food bowl twenty

minutes after his meal, giving him enough time to eat but not enough time to bury a snack. Avoid giving your dog bones altogether.

How to Deter Digging

If the suggestions in this book don't work or can't be applied to your situation, the next step is to make digging a less desirable activity for your dog. There are a number of ways you can accomplish this.

Start by observing your dog, either in person or with the use of a video camera. Observing your dog will help you figure out the exact moment when your dog starts digging—information that can help you devise a solution. For instance, if you notice that your dog starts to dig after he's been left outside for half an hour, bring him inside in twenty-five minutes. This should help short-circuit the digging behavior.

The most positive method to stop digging requires your presence. Any time you see your dog start to dig, make an unpleasant noise, such as "Aaaack," to get his attention. When he stops digging, call him to you and give him a treat for coming, or grab his favorite toy and play with him. The intent is to make being with you more fun than digging.

To deter digging along the fence line, bury chicken wire at the base of the fence (with the sharp edges rolled under) or place large rocks along the bottom of the fence line. If you're installing a fence for the first time, bury the bottom

of the fence one to two feet underground, or lay chain link fencing on the ground and anchor it to the bottom of the fence. This makes it uncomfortable for your dog to walk near the fence. Keep in mind, however, that these tactics won't prevent your dog from digging elsewhere in the yard.

When your dog digs in a particular spot or digs to escape, make the area unpleasant for digging by placing rocks, gravel, bricks, pinecones, or aluminum foil in the hole, or by placing chicken wire in the dirt. None of these are pleasant digging

surfaces for dogs. For a very wide hole, try placing a metal or plastic garbage can lid inside the hole and covering it with dirt. The noise a dog's paws make against the lid and the feel of metal or plastic may deter your digger.

You may also want to consider installing an electronic containment system that surrounds the forbidden space. While many of these systems deter a dog with an electronic shock, a new version gives off a burst of citronella spray whenever a dog wearing the collar that relays a signal to the system crosses the boundary. Citronella, a fragrant grass whose oil is often used in insect repellent, is not harmful, but dogs don't like its scent. This collar is less severe than a shock collar and tends to be more effective.

Another tactic is to fill the holes with substances that are unappealing to a dog's taste buds or sense of smell. Stuff a hole with newspaper, and then sprinkle on alum, cayenne pepper, or hot sauce. The digging dog who gets a whiff or taste of these substances may think twice before beginning his next excavation project.

Electric fencing is a last resort. A low-voltage hot wire can be buried underground, around the perimeter of a fence. While an electric shock is painful, some trainers and humane organizations believe a minor shock is better for a dog than escaping and getting lost or hit by a car. Ask your trainer or behaviorist, recommended by your veterinarian, for his or her advice before installing this type of device.

Unfortunately, not every dog is deterred by these tactics. Some dogs simply view them as a challenge to overcome.

Correcting Digging Behavior

Interaction and observation is required to stop digging dogs in their tracks. First, you need to spend time with your dog and keep him entertained so that he doesn't want to dig. When you show interest in your dog, he won't resort to misbehavior for your attention. Knowing why and when your dog digs will help you eliminate his motivation for digging and redirect his digging to a

more appropriate place or behavior. It's especially important that you pay close attention to your dog's outdoor activities during the first year and a half of his life. If you teach him when he's young that digging isn't permitted or that digging is permitted only in certain places, your life will be much easier.

Second, you need to correct your dog every time you catch him in the act. Any time your dog is out in the yard, use a remote correction device such as a shake can (a clean empty soda can filled with noisemakers such as pebbles or pennies with the lid taped over so the noisemakers don't fall out). Whenever you see your dog digging, toss the can in his direction (don't hit him with it). If possible, don't let your dog see you throw the can. The noise, which should seem to come from nowhere, will startle him so that he stops digging. Distract him by giving him a toy to play with or by taking him to the preferred digging area.

A similar correction involves the use of a water hose or squirt gun. Whenever you see your dog digging, squirt him and say, "No dig." Follow this with the distraction of a toy or the introduction to a place where it's okay to dig. When he's behaving praise him by saying, "Good no dig."

If you prefer *not* to use a shake can or water correction, simply yell, "No dig!" When he stops, praise him, give him a toy, play a game with him, or show him where he can dig. When you follow a correction with something pleasant, your dog will want to pay attention to you and follow your command.

Some dogs learn to tune out the word no because they hear it so frequently. If this is the case with your dog, get his attention by substituting it with a harsh sound like that of a game show buzzer, "Aaaaght."

Finally, catch your dog doing something right. Whenever you notice that he's not digging, praise him for whatever he is doing, "Good Max to chew on your toy," or "Good Max to play with your ball."

There are a number of corrections that are effective without being cruel. Harsh physical punishment such as hitting a dog after the fact or filling a hole with water and sticking a dog's head in it is not only abusive, but it also doesn't address the cause of the behavior or help you to form a bond with your dog. Any kind of harsh punishment can also cause dogs to become fearful or anxious or do their digging in secret. Harsh punishment doesn't communicate to your dog the reason you're punishing him; he cannot associate your anger with the hole that he's dug.

Not every solution in this book is effective with every dog. Be patient, and try different things until something works. And remember, your dog's behavior is linked to the environment and training you give him.

Barking

Why Do Dogs Bark?

Dogs bark for any number of reasons. They bark when someone approaches their territory, in response to other dogs, and sometimes in response to noises, such as sirens. They bark at squirrels and other potential prey. Some breeds are born to bark; it's in their nature. Often dogs bark in excitement, such as when they know they are going for a walk, taking a car ride, or getting their dinner. Occasionally, barking is stress related, a sign of separation anxiety. Sometimes dogs bark just because they're bored.

Researchers have found that dogs almost always have a reason for barking. Barking is a complex means of close-range communication, and dogs make a number of basic vocal sounds. Their barks often express various emotions, such as loneliness, fear, distress, and pleasure. For instance, a stressed dog—say, one who's left home alone—has a high-pitched, atonal, repetitive bark. Noisy barks are usually defensive in nature, while harmonic barks occur in play and other social contexts.

Just as people in different parts of the world have different accents and languages, different dog breeds have subtle variations in their types of barks. These variations are believed to correspond to dialects. And even the sounds people use to describe dog barks vary from country to country, from *woof-woof* in English to *jau-jau* in Spanish to *wung-wung* in Chinese. Is this because our dogs are

speaking different languages, or are we simply not paying careful attention to what they're saying?

If you pay close attention to your dog, you can learn to decipher her different barks. To get you started, here are some "translations" from canine ethologists (people who study dog behavior):

- A rapid string of three or four barks with pauses between each series means, "Let's get together. There's something we need to check out."

- Rapid barking at a midrange pitch is an alarm meant to alert other dogs or people. It usually occurs when a stranger enters the territory.

- Continuous barking at a slower pace and lower pitch than the alarm bark indicates an immediate threat.

- Bark and pause, bark and pause, bark and pause for a long period of time indicates a dog is lonely.

- One or two short, sharp barks is a typical canine greeting.

- A single loud bark means, "Knock it off!" Dogs

often do this when they're awakened from a nice nap or their tail is tugged by a playful puppy.

- Puppies use insistent barks to get attention.
- Some dogs learn to call their owners when it's dinnertime or when they'd like to go outside. They usually do this with a single, purposeful bark.
- A dog whose bark rises in level of intensity is excited or having a good time.

Who Barks and Why?

Some dog breeds have been bred to bark. Perhaps the most well-known barking breeds are the terriers. These specialized hunting dogs, whose original purpose was to follow their prey into underground dens or burrows, needed to have some way of letting their people know where they were in case they got stuck underground. Barking was much more effective than, say, collars with bells, which had the drawback of getting stuck on roots underground and were sometimes difficult to hear. People who kept terriers for hunting began selecting dogs who barked loudly when they were excited. They bred them with other dogs who had this trait, and before long, all terriers were barkers. Other breeds that tend to bark a lot include beagles, keeshonden, cocker spaniels, and herding breeds, such as Shetland sheepdogs.

The basenji, on the other hand, is known as the barkless breed. The basenji does make noise, although the sound is usually described as a soft howling or yodeling. It's not that basenjis can't

bark; they just seldom do so unless they're terribly excited. Why don't basenjis bark? We don't know, but it may be that silence was safer for dogs in the African wilds, where the basenji first originated. It may also simply be a genetic trait for this particular breed.

The tendency to bark is very likely the result of a dominant gene. When dogs who don't bark much are bred with dogs who bark a lot, puppies are much more likely to bark than not bark. Researchers have not found whether female dogs bark more than male dogs or vice versa. Purebreds and mutts are equally likely to bark excessively.

Dogs can also learn to bark from each other. A dog who has learned to bark appropriately is invaluable in teaching a new puppy what kind of bark is necessary for asking to be let outside or how long to bark when people come to the door. However, a nuisance barker can teach bad habits to a new dog. And just as humans sometimes pick up the accent of the place where they live, dogs can learn to copy the intonations of other dogs' barks.

When Barking Becomes a Problem

The most important thing to know about barking is that it is a normal dog behavior. At appropriate times and levels, barking is even considered to be a useful behavior. Many people get dogs because they want them to bark when someone is either coming to the door or prowling around at night. But when barking becomes excessive, the noise can be a real headache for owners and their long-suffering neighbors. According to the Cornell Animal Behavior Clinic, up to one-third of behavioral complaints involve nuisance, inappropriate, or excessive barking.

Before things get out of hand, take steps to teach your dog when it's okay to bark and when she should stop or remain quiet. If you want her to bark when people approach the house, enlist your kids, spouse, or a neighbor to help with the training. Ask the helper to come to the door and knock or ring the doorbell. If your dog doesn't bark at the noise, encourage her by excitedly asking, "Who's there? Is someone at the door?" Praise your dog when she barks at the sound.

Once your dog is barking to alert you, the next step is to teach her when to stop. After she has given a couple of barks, hold up your hand and say a code word or command, such as *enough* or *quiet*. Give the command in a firm, quiet tone of voice. If you yell, your dog will simply think you're barking back at her, and she'll just bark more. If your dog stops barking, praise her—"good quiet!"—and pop a treat into her mouth. Be sure you give the praise and treat only when the dog is quiet.

Often, showing the dog a treat may be distraction enough to stop the barking. Say, "quiet," and give her the treat after several seconds of silence. As your dog starts to learn what the word *quiet* means, extend the amount of time between saying the command and giving the reward.

Some trainers recommend wrapping your hand around your barking dog's muzzle, or snout, and

saying, "quiet" or "no bark." That works some-times, but you have to be careful when trying that technique. If your dog is barking frenziedly, she may accidentally bite you when you try to wrap your hand around her muzzle.

A safer way to get this effect is to keep a halter collar on your dog while you're at home. This type of collar has a loop that wraps around your dog's muzzle. When your dog barks more than once or twice, give a quick pull on the lead to tighten the loop around the muzzle. As soon as the dog is quiet, say, "good no bark" or "good quiet," and reward her with a treat.

Another way to stop the barking is to call your dog to you or give her a *down* command. Calling your dog to you usually interrupts barking. And a dog hardly ever barks when lying down. Choose a command such as *come* or *down* and use the same one every time. Offer praise for silence and then reward your dog with a treat.

Be sure you don't unintentionally reward your dog for barking by hugging her or saying soothingly,

"It's okay, Sweetie." When you do that, the dog thinks she must have been right to bark. This simply encourages her to bark more the next time a similar situation occurs.

Solving a Barking Problem

When you're trying to retrain a dog who barks excessively, the first step is to figure out why she is barking. Dogs are social animals, and most often, excessive barking occurs when they're left outdoors all the time with little human contact and nothing to occupy them. If your dog is bored or anxious, punishment is not an appropriate response to the barking. The solution is to understand why she's bored or anxious and deal with the problem. You might find that your dog is seeking attention or even trying to defend her territory. Videotaping the dog while you're gone can help you figure out at what point barking starts, as well as what sets it off.

The most important way you can solve barking problems resulting from boredom is to let your dog inside the house, especially when you're at home. Teach your dog to act appropriately in the house so she can live with you instead of being tied out in the backyard. That's no life for a dog.

There are times in every dog's life, though, when she needs to stay alone. Help make these times bearable by providing interactive toys such as Kongs and Buster Cubes, which can be filled with food. Hide the toys around the house so your dog

has to work to find them. One innovative trainer recommends packing a "sack lunch" for your dog. Fill a paper bag with treats and toys, tape it up, then leave it for your dog to get into on her own. She'll spend her time trying to get at the treats instead of barking her head off. To prevent boredom, rotate the toys and vary the types of treats you use. Occasionally, substitute cream cheese for peanut butter or liver biscuits for cheese-flavored mini bones.

Exercise is an important part of relieving boredom. Walk the dog or play fetch before you leave.

If possible, have a neighbor or pet-sitter come in during the day to help break up the monotony with a walk or a little playtime.

Anxiety is a common cause of problem barking. Anxious dogs, like bored dogs, are usually lonely. It's important to help these dogs learn to relax through behavior modification. Start by getting your dog used to being left alone for short periods. Put your dog in her crate with a treat. Don't make a fuss about leaving; instead, be matter-of-fact about it. Stay away for only a minute or two so your dog doesn't have time to become anxious and start barking. Gradually extend the amount of time you leave the dog alone. Make sure she has a toy to play with, and consider leaving the radio or television on so she can hear human voices.

A crate serves as a valuable tool for helping anxious dogs. Crated dogs are cozy and comfortable in their special place, freed of the responsibilities of being on their own. Dogs who are rewarded with a treat for entering their crate often are delighted when they hear the word *crate* and race to see who can get there first. Outdoor dogs may

find a similar sense of security if they have access to a doghouse or are confined to a dog run.

Another way to help reduce anxiety is to vary your routine before leaving. Dogs quickly pick up on visual cues, such as putting on a coat or pulling keys out of a purse. Change your routine by doing things in a different order or going through the motions but then staying home. Eventually, your dog will learn to ignore these cues and relax.

Behavior modification takes time, so be patient. In severe barking cases, a veterinary behaviorist may have to prescribe medication to smooth out the process. Medication isn't a quick fix, though, and won't solve the problem without behavior modification.

Some dogs just won't shut up. They love hearing the sound of their own voice, and once they get started, they don't stop. If your dog simply won't quit barking when people come to the door—or in other situations when you're present—and you haven't had any success with training, use of a crate, behavior modification, and plenty of family interaction and exercise, you may need to turn up the intensity.

If your dog keeps barking, give her a loud verbal signal—"Aaaack!" or "No!"—followed by a correction, such as a squirt of water from a spray bottle or tossing a throw pillow or a shake can (made by placing a few pennies in a clean, empty soda can and taping over the top) in her direction. Don't hit your dog with the objects. The goal of these actions is to make your dog realize that prolonged barking has unpleasant consequences. You need to teach your dog that you are in control of the situation. Once she has alerted you, she needs to be quiet and let you take over.

Dogs often bark too much when they want attention. The best way to deal with an attention-seeker is to ignore the barking. This is especially important with a puppy, whom you need to teach early on that you won't respond until she *stops* barking.

Dogs may also bark because they want something. They want to eat, they want to go out, or they want to play. It's important to make sure that your dog doesn't train you to respond to her barked demands. Always wait until she has been quiet for at least thirty seconds before you give her what she wants, such as giving her a meal, letting her out of her crate or into the yard, or tossing her ball. If you give in even once, your dog will have learned that she can manipulate you by barking, and it will take a long time to retrain her.

If you can see a pattern to the barking, take steps to break it. For instance, if your dog barks at the same time every morning because she wants

out of her crate, wake up a few minutes early (before she starts barking), take her outside to do her business, then put her back in her crate, and go back to bed. Ignore further barking (wear earplugs if you have to). Your dog will learn that barking will not get her any kind of attention whatsoever.

It's very important to ignore attention-seeking barking. Walk away from the dog if you have to, but don't yell at her or thump the top of her crate. That simply gives the dog the response she wants, even though it's a negative response. When your

dog finally does stop, be sure to give her an extra special reward: a favorite game or a tasty treat.

Excitable dogs who bark nonstop during play simply need a chance to calm down. Bring down the intensity of the game or take a break from play until the dog is under control. If a squirrel or a bird triggers the behavior, take the dog inside. When she's quiet, start the game again. Your behavior will teach your dog that too much barking puts an end to the good times.

Dogs are extremely observant, and they learn quickly that barking at strangers seems to drive them away. So a dog who's allowed to stand at the door or run along the fence and bark at people has her behavior reinforced frequently when people walk by the house or when mail carriers stuff the mailbox and then depart. *I bark; they leave,* the dog thinks. If this type of barking is permitted without correction, it can lead to territorial aggression.

You can prevent problems by teaching your dog to look to you for guidance when strangers

approach. Correct her when she barks at people who are merely walking by the house, and have your mail carriers and delivery people work with you to teach your dog not to bark at them. Provide the "stranger" with treats and ask him or her to approach you and the dog. As long as the dog remains quiet, the person can toss treats to the dog, while otherwise ignoring her. Once the dog has relaxed and is no longer showing interest in barking at the person, you and the dog can walk away. This can also work if your dog barks at approaching people while you're out for a walk. Set up a similar situation with a friend or neighbor.

Go slowly with this type of training. You want your dog to learn to trust your judgment and to feel comfortable in the presence of accepted strangers. It may take days or weeks of work before you achieve this.

If You Want Your Dog to Act As a Watchdog

Teaching your dog what *not* to bark at is the first step in developing watchdog abilities. If your dog always barks at squirrels or birds or the mail carrier, she'll never develop any discrimination, and you'll never know when to pay attention to her barking. Keep in mind as well that proper alarm barking may not develop until the dog is mature, at eighteen months to two years of age.

A good watchdog barks only when someone is attempting to enter the house or in the presence of dangerous situations, such as fires. Pay attention to what your dog barks at so you can correct

promiscuous barking and praise watchdog barking. Set up situations to help teach your dog when
barking is appropriate. For instance, ask a friend
or neighbor to approach the house stealthily and
try to enter the backdoor. Encourage your dog to
bark when she hears this type of noise and praise
her when she complies.

Be Patient

Just as when you're teaching any other behavior, training a dog to be quiet requires a lot of practice. Set up situations that give you the opportunity to show your dog what you want from her. Keep training sessions short—no more than five or ten minutes at a time. And no matter what techniques you use, be sure the entire family understands them and does them the same way (for example, use the same commands and praise, and be sure that everyone praises the same

behaviors consistently). Consistency is one of the keys to teaching dogs successfully. It takes a while to teach a dog to be quiet on command, so don't give up. You didn't learn algebra in a day but in a semester or two; your dog requires plenty of learning time as well.

Bark-Control Devices

When a dog's barking is out of control and no training methods have worked to stop the barking, a bark-control collar, sometimes called an anti-bark collar, may help. This type of collar uses electronic shock, a spray of citronella scent, or sound to get the dog's attention and let her know that her behavior is unacceptable.

The correction stops when the barking does. This type of training device works best when used in combination with other behavior modification tools, such as rewarding the dog when she's being quiet and familiarizing her with the types of sounds and circumstances that cause barking, such as ringing doorbells or telephones. Do not consider a bark-control collar to be a quick fix. It's important to figure out why your dog is barking and to work on eliminating the cause or changing the dog's response to the cause. For instance, if the neighborhood kids are teasing your dog, ask them to stop or train the dog to behave differently if it continues.

How well a bark-control collar works depends in large part on the dog's personality as well as on the owner's training skills. Bad timing or incorrect use of the collar can make the situation worse. This is especially true of electronic, or shock, collars. Dogs who are extremely timid, sensitive, or noise-shy may react negatively to the unexpected sound, feel, or scent of a bark-control collar.

Most respected dog trainers recommend against using electronic-shock training devices, which deliver an irritating shock of adjustable intensity when a vibration sensor in the collar detects barking. The potential is high for misuse and abuse of these devices. Before buying an electronic collar,

consider trying the device on yourself before you use it on your dog. You may change your mind about using one.

The best choice is a collar that gives a correction using sound or a spray of citronella mist. Citronella is a fragrant grass whose oil is often used in insect repellent. Its scent is irritating but harmless. This type of collar works by releasing a spray of citronella scent whenever a microphone in the collar detects the sound of barking. In a study done at Cornell University's College of

Veterinary Medicine, citronella collars were more effective than shock collars in reducing or stopping nuisance barking.

Spray collars are less aversive than shock collars and are a good first step when other methods fail to remedy nuisance barking. Don't just put the collar on your dog and leave, though. It's better to be there the first time your dog experiences the spray. Some dogs may be frightened and start to bark repeatedly, quickly using up the spray. Over time, some dogs may even learn not to bark when

the collar is on but will then start barking again once the collar is off.

Sound-correction collars send out a high-decibel noise when the dog barks, serving as both an interruption and a correction. A microphone on the collar should ensure that the dog is corrected for only her own barking, not that of any other dog, and the collar should be programmable to a particular dog's level of barking. Some collars allow the owner to choose the number of barks permitted before the sound correction is set off.

No matter which collar you choose, it's best to seek advice from a qualified animal behaviorist, dog trainer, or veterinary behaviorist to find out if the product is appropriate and how to use it. This is especially true if you're a first-time user or an inexperienced dog owner. Choose a trainer who considers all other options first and who has a humane sensibility. Begin at the lowest level, and increase the collar's intensity only if necessary. Oftentimes, it only takes a couple of corrections at the lowest level to solve the problem.

Before you buy any product of this type, make sure it has safety features that prevent the collar from being misused. Such features include adjustable levels of correction and automatic shut-off so the dog isn't continually corrected. If you decide to use a shock collar, the packaging should indicate that all parts of the device are UL-certified, meaning they have passed electrical safety tests.

Ask about the availability of technical assistance either by phone from the manufacturer's customer service department or from a local sales representative. For any type of bark-control collar, the product should have complete and easy-to-understand instructions that focus on how to change rather than control the dog's behavior. And remember that the use of such a device can cause anxious dogs to become even more nervous, making the problem worse. Some bark-control collars serve as valuable tools if they're used correctly, but they won't put an end to nuisance barking without behavior modification or eliminating the causes of boredom and anxiety.

Puppy Preschool

If your dog is a puppy, now is the time to start her off on the right paw by keeping her from developing bad habits in puppyhood. The little yapper might be cute at three months, but her noisemaking won't be cute at six months. To keep problem barking at bay, introduce your puppy to different people and expose her regularly to all kinds of sounds: vacuum cleaners, doorbells, traffic, and so on. As your dog grows older and gets used to encountering a variety of noises, people, and situations, she'll learn what requires a bark and when silence is golden.

Aggression

What Is Aggression?

Aggression is the most common problem canine behaviorists see. Why is it so common? The reason is simple: aggression is a normal behavior for dogs. One of the many ways dogs communicate is through actions, including threats and attacks, directed toward people or other animals. Problems with aggression occur when there's miscommunication between people and dogs—not surprising since we don't speak the same language.

Can any dog be aggressive? Yes, from toy breeds to terriers, any dog has the potential for aggression. But like it or not, some breeds are more likely than others to have aggressive tendencies. Terriers, for instance, have all been bred for aggression toward small, furry prey animals such as moles, badgers, and rats. When the terrier's natural prey is unavailable, this aggressive tendency can easily be turned toward cats or pocket pets such as hamsters and gerbils. Dogs who are bred to guard property or livestock have a genetic

tendency toward aggression. It's a normal part of being a guard dog. Because there's genetic variability within each breed, some dogs within a breed can have a higher genetic tendency to be aggressive than others of the same breed. Because aggression is heritable, dogs who show inappropriate aggressive behavior should be spayed or neutered so they don't pass on the tendency to their offspring.

Even though aggression is a normal behavior for dogs, it doesn't mean it should be permitted. Dogs live in a human environment and they need to learn to behave properly in that setting. It's important to understand that a dog's perceptions influence his aggressive behavior, but it's also important for dogs to be able to adjust to their living situation. In the following chapters, we'll see how to identify aggression, recognize and prevent different types of aggression, and seek solutions to aggression problems.

What Does Aggression Look Like?

Some people bring their dog to a behaviorist for being aggressive when the dog's merely jumping up on people. Jumping up is bad manners, but it's not necessarily an aggressive behavior unless the behavior is accompanied by another physical sign. An aggressive dog gives threat signals by curling his lips, baring his teeth, growling, barking threateningly, snapping, or biting. These behaviors can be directed toward people or other animals. When a dog is jumping up on someone and displaying one or more of these signals, then you have an aggressive dog.

Canine body language isn't always clear. For instance, dogs often bare their teeth in a smile or growl in play. How can you tell the difference between playing and aggressive posturing? Look at the dog's body language. If the dog's lip retracts upward (vertically) and his body is stiff and quivering, watch out! If the lip retracts horizontally and the dog's tail is wagging, it's generally a friendly smile.

The same is true of play growls. A puppy who lifts his lip and growls while staring at you isn't showing any intent to play. On the other hand, if he's in a play bow (rear up in the air, tail wagging, head down, smiling up at you) with a happy face, you can be reasonably sure the pup is inviting you

to join in on a game. Playful growls or excited bark-ing often accompany the play bow. Once you learn how to watch dogs, you can see a clear difference between play and aggression with intent to harm. Think of it this way: if the behavior makes you want to back away from the dog—it's aggression.

Bully Boy or Fearful Fido?

Aggression can be placed in three broad cate-gories: aggression toward owners, aggression toward strangers, and aggression toward other animals. Each has a variety of potential causes, although when you get right down to it, the main motivation for all is some form of fear.

Dogs may be aggressive toward their people because they don't understand their place in the family "pack" or they're afraid a new family mem-ber such as a baby or a new spouse threatens their place in the pack. This is often called domi-nance aggression, although some behaviorists are moving away from that term. Instead, they refer to it as conflict aggression because many dogs who are described as dominant also show fear. When we use the term dominant, it makes us more likely to punish a dog, which is counterproductive.

A dog with conflict aggression often hasn't learned that you and other family members are in charge and therefore tries to claim the role of leader of the pack. He might growl if asked to move off the furniture or if any attempt is made to restrain him. This dog doesn't like having his head patted

because he views it as an aggressive move. You should suspect this type of aggression if your dog displays body language such as standing tall and staring at you or snarling. Other signs of conflict aggression include guarding food or favorite toys; snarling or snapping when told no! or when being handled for any reason; and being overprotective of a particular family member. Conflict aggression usually appears during adolescence and young adulthood, which ranges from one to three years of age.

Other dogs may show aggression toward their owners because they're afraid or they associate the owner with a frightening experience—one the owner might not even be aware of. A fearful dog is often this way because he wasn't socialized properly as a puppy. It's easy to tell if a dog is fearful by reading his body language. Fearful dogs slink, crouch, shake, or cower. Don't be fooled by this behavior! If you reach for a dog and he feels cornered, he may bite. Punishment for this behavior can make a dog become even more fearful, continuing the cycle of aggression.

Dogs who are aggressive toward strangers usually behave that way because they're defending their territory, which could be the house, the yard, or the car. If your dog urine-marks—lifts his leg on trees, walls, or other objects—when you go for walks around the block, he may view the whole neighborhood as his territory. Territorial aggression is especially common when your dog is faced with either unexpected or unknown people or animals.

Another type of territorial aggression is protective aggression. Protective aggression occurs when your dog is aggressive toward strangers because he thinks he needs to protect you from an approaching stranger, especially one on an unfamiliar vehicle such as a bicycle or a skateboard. You can put the bite on territorial aggression by taking your new puppy to puppy kindergarten classes. You can start this when your puppy is as young as 10 weeks old.

When a young dog is exposed early on to lots of other people and dogs, he is less likely to become territorially aggressive.

Fear can also cause aggression toward strangers. For instance, your dog may be fearful at the veterinary clinic or grooming shop. That's why it's always a good idea for you and your dog to first visit the vet or groomer just for fun, without any painful vaccinations or scary blow dryers.

Aggression toward other animals might involve a dispute over dominance among dogs in the same household or predatory aggression toward prey animals such as cats, squirrels, or birds. Terriers love to chase cats and squirrels, and spaniels and retrievers have been known to watch pet birds for hours, waiting for a chance to pounce. Some behaviorists say this type of predatory behavior isn't really aggression at all because it's only natural for dogs—especially certain breeds—to want to catch and eat prey; you might say it's bred in the bone. Because predatory behavior is so strong in some dogs, prevention is more important than

treatment. The only way to prevent predatory behavior is to limit the dog's opportunities to give chase. Keep your dog on a leash and under control any time there's a chance he might encounter a cat or other prey animal that you don't want him to chase.

Other Types of Aggression

Some behaviorists break aggression down further, depending on how or to whom the behavior is displayed. The following are some of the many ways aggression is described. As with the types of aggression discussed earlier, they all relate back to fear in one way or another.

Possessive aggression occurs when dogs guard objects such as food, toys, or anything else they value. It's closely related to territorial and protective

aggression. This is one of the easier forms of aggression to manage, which you can do by teaching your dog that good things come when he gives up a toy or food bowl without a fight. First you combine taking an item away with giving something back. For instance, a behaviorist might recommend first adding food to your dog's dish, then taking the dish away, adding more food, and giving the dish back. The dog learns that good things happen when people touch his food dish. You can also teach your dog that if he gives up or drops a toy, another toy or a food treat appears.

Maternal aggression is the protective behavior of a mother in defense of her pups. A dog may growl or otherwise act aggressively when strangers—or even favorite family members—approach her new puppies. Maternal aggression usually disappears once pups are weaned. In the meantime, though, it's important to teach Mom that it's okay for people to handle her babies, providing positive reinforcement every time she lets people approach and touch her pups.

Maternal aggression is usually seen during the first three weeks after the mother dog gives birth. If she shows aggression when strangers are around, keep them away during this time. If the aggression continues after three weeks, take your dog to another room when people come to visit or take the puppies to the visitor. Puppies need socialization from people other than family members, so don't give in to maternal aggression.

Fear aggression is defensive in nature. A dog who thinks he's in danger will try to either defend himself or run—the "fight or flight" response. Dogs who haven't been well socialized might mistake innocent actions—the fast-moving hand of a toddler or an arm raised to throw a ball—as attacks and act to defend themselves by growling or biting. When they see that their behavior gets the reaction they want—a person backs off—a pattern is set. Fear aggression is often described as a kind of anxiety disorder and is treated as such. Sometimes drug therapy may help.

Pain-related aggression is exactly what it sounds like. Just as we might yell at someone who handles us roughly when we don't feel good, dogs with

injuries or health problems may growl or bite when they're touched in a sore spot. Dogs who do this need to learn that touch is rewarding, not painful. Be careful any time you touch a dog in pain, and make sure your dog has plenty of handling from puppyhood on. He should be used to having you groom him, touch his feet, and look in his mouth. Teach him to let other people touch him as well. It makes it easier for veterinarians and groomers to do their jobs.

Who Ya Gonna Call?

If your dog shows signs of aggression, don't shrug it off. Aggression is a serious problem that should be dealt with immediately before the dog becomes dangerous. A single bite can scar a child for life and a more vicious attack can kill a person. In some communities, a single bite—even if it's relatively harmless—can result in the dog being euthanized. Teaching a dog to interact appropriately with people is one of a dog owner's highest responsibilities. Don't hesitate to seek professional help in countering aggressive tendencies. And until you can get help, avoid situations that seem to provoke your dog's aggressive behavior.

Begin by taking your dog to the veterinarian to rule out pain-related aggression. Your veterinarian can perform a physical exam and run lab tests to make sure your dog isn't unhealthy or in pain from an injury. If your dog is healthy, ask your veterinarian for a referral to a behaviorist. The vet may recommend a board-certified veterinary behaviorist—a vet who specializes in animal behavior—or an applied animal behaviorist certified through the Applied Animal Behavior Society. Another way to find qualified help is to contact the American Veterinary Society of Animal Behavior at www.avma.org/avsab/ for a referral.

Even if you get a referral, look for signs that the behaviorist is up-to-date on the latest thinking in dog behavior. For instance, run from anyone who recommends alpha rolls—holding the dog on his back and staring at him—or other dominance behaviors to put the dog in his place. Alpha rolls

and similar techniques are outmoded. Punishment and domination techniques almost always make aggression worse because they increase the level of fear in an already fearful dog.

Developing a treatment plan for a behavioral problem involves obtaining an accurate behavioral history to reach a precise diagnosis. At your first meeting, the behaviorist will ask you what triggers your dog's aggressive behavior. It's important that you don't leave anything out. Even minor details can help the behaviorist determine an accurate diagnosis. Depending on the diagnosis, behavior modification, environmental adjustments, or some-times drug therapy is used to treat the aggression.

Dealing with Aggression

Behavior modification under the guidance of a qualified behaviorist is the best way to reprogram an aggressive dog. Behavior modification involves changing the dog's environment, changing the

dog's behavior through training or operant condi-
tioning (the association formed between a behavior and a consequence), or changing the dog's
brain chemistry through use of drugs. Behaviorists
use a variety of techniques to help dogs understand their place in the family and to learn to
accept you as the leader.

These techniques include desensitizing the dog
to whatever causes his fear or to the targets of the
dog's aggression; withdrawing or rationing attention; teaching the dog that family members are the
source of all good things; reducing the dog's sense
of importance; obedience training; use of training

tools such as head collars; and spaying or neutering. Be aware that there's no "one size fits all" solution. A behaviorist tailors methods to the individual dog and family situation as well as to the type of aggression. Let's take a look at one of the ways the various types of aggression might be handled.

Avoidance is the first step when treating many types of aggression. This means changing or avoiding anything that triggers the behavior. For instance, if your dog reacts aggressively when his head is patted, don't pat his head.

Why does avoidance work? It works because your dog can no longer use those situations to manipulate you and isn't being rewarded for misbehavior. And a reward is exactly what happens when you back away from your dog or stop requiring him to do something he doesn't want to do. Once your dog's ability to manipulate matters to his satisfaction is removed, behavior modification techniques can be used to change his actions and teach him to live compatibly with you and other family members.

Changing a Dog's Behavior

Behavior modification techniques can be passive or active. Passive techniques don't involve any kind of force or physical manipulation. They include ignoring the dog (no touching, or other attention); requiring the dog to work for attention or food; and not permitting the dog on any furniture or to jump up on people. All of these techniques communicate to the dog that he's no longer in charge.

How do they work? The behaviorist might start by advising you to ignore all of your dog's attempts to get your attention, such as nosing you for petting, placing a paw on your knee, or bringing a toy for play. Dogs love attention, so when it's withdrawn, they sit up and take notice.

Once you've established a pattern of withholding attention—which might take a week or two—the behaviorist might recommend that you begin to offer attention on your own terms. For instance, the behaviorist might recommend that you occasionally respond to your dog's requests for attention by first requiring him to perform a command such as *sit* or *down*. When the dog complies, give him praise, pets, and a treat. Soon your dog will learn that rewards come with calm, attentive behavior. Even young puppies can learn to sit still for a few seconds and pay attention to their people when they discover that the reward is attention or food.

When you require a dog to sit or lie down before you pet him, feed him, or take him for a

walk, you establish yourself as the leader. You can further establish your leadership by not letting your dog sleep on the bed, lie on furniture, or jump up on people. How can you avoid these behaviors? Take jumping up, for instance. When your dog does this, simply pivot so he misses you and then walk away. An alternative to walking away is to give the *sit* command. When the dog sits, then he gets attention.

Supervising and restricting where the dog goes are other forms of passive behavior modification. For instance, a dog who chases people or other animals in a predatory way should be confined to a yard or kept on a leash so he can't act on his instincts. Never leave this type of dog alone with babies, toddlers, or young children. In fact, no dog should ever be left unsupervised with young children.

Active behavior modification involves the use of training tools such as head collars, obedience

training classes, and desensitization and counter-conditioning techniques. A head collar, similar to a horse halter, allows you to control your dog's head and helps reduce pulling on walks. It's an effective, harmless way to communicate to your dog what you want. When your dog walks nicely, then he gets praise.

Obedience training reinforces that the person is in charge. Teaching your dog to respond to commands enables you to interrupt aggressive acts and replace them with positive actions for which the dog can be rewarded. *Sit* and *down* commands are especially useful because they place the dog in a submissive position. Practice obedience work, accompanied by such positive rewards as treats, toys, or play, daily throughout your dog's life. Always end training sessions on a high note, and never ask a dog to do something he's not fully capable of achieving.

Once your dog reliably performs obedience commands—especially the *stay* command—the behaviorist may introduce desensitization and counterconditioning sessions. Desensitization and counterconditioning work by gradually exposing the dog to things that previously caused aggressive behavior and rewarding him for tolerating them. This way, the dog slowly learns to accept, strangers, cats, or whatever else he fears or dislikes. During these sessions, a muzzle may be necessary to prevent bites.

Territorial aggression is a good example of how desensitization and counterconditioning might be used. A common way of dealing with territorial aggression is to place your dog on a leash and require him to sit every time someone walks by your house. Praise him and give a treat every time he complies. Then have the dog sit, and reward him as a family member approaches the door and knocks. When this is accepted, ask a familiar neighbor to approach and knock. Repeat the sit-and-reward sequence each time he complies. Finally, work with the dog as a stranger approaches and knocks at the door. The goal is for the dog to welcome the arrival of people because he associates

their approach with a treat or some other reward.

Whether recommending active or passive behavior modification techniques, the behaviorist should demonstrate everything he or she asks you to do. Don't be afraid to ask questions if you don't understand something. You should also consider keeping a diary of your dog's behavior. This will help you recognize patterns and see changes. Sometimes it doesn't seem as if a dog is improving, but a look at the diary may show significant improvement so gradual that it wasn't even noticed.

Can Drugs Help?

Almost all of us would like to be able to cure problems with a pill, but medication isn't the best or most effective treatment for a complex behavior such as aggression. Drug therapy is useful for some types of aggression but not for all, and it must always be combined with behavior modification. Drugs such as Prozac and Valium have their place in dealing with behavior problems, but they're not cure-alls. There's always a risk that drugs can make aggression worse. Drugs are expensive and since the amount of the drug given is based on a dog's size, it can cost more to treat medium-size and large dogs than small dogs. Be aware, too, that none of the drugs currently prescribed for aggression is approved for that use.

That said, drug therapy has its uses from short-term relief of anxiety during behavior modification to long-term use for hard-core cases. Several types of drugs may be prescribed for aggression. They include anxiolytics (drugs that relieve

anxiety) such as buspirone or tricyclic antidepressants; specific serotonin reuptake inhibitors—SSRIs—which may reduce aggressive or impulsive behavior; or synthetic progestins, which are sometimes useful in dealing with conflict or territorial aggression but have long-term side effects.

It's important to remember that drugs aren't necessarily a quick fix. It can take six to eight weeks before any change appears in your dog's behavior. Some behaviorists recommend behavior modification before introducing drugs. That way they can see what's working and have a better idea of whether drugs can be useful.

Diet and Exercise

Diet and exercise may well be factors in dealing with aggression, and you can make some easy changes that might help reduce your dog's aggression. Since food allergies can cause behavior problems and irritability, begin by taking a look at your dog's diet. First give your dog a food with different ingredients, ideally ingredients that your dog hasn't eaten before, such as duck, turkey, or venison. Check the label on dog treats. Many are high in sugar, salt, and preservatives, which some dogs are sensitive to.

If your dog eats a diet that is high in protein—a source of energy—but leads a couch potato lifestyle, diet combined with lack of exercise may be the problem. Ask your veterinarian to recom-

mend high-quality foods that are lower in protein. Then add some exercise to your dog's life. Putting him out in the back yard to play just doesn't cut it. Taking long walks, jogging, and playing interactively with you—fetching a tennis ball or chasing a Frisbee—are musts if you want your dog to be physically and emotionally healthy.

What Not to Do

Never hit your dog. It's never okay to beat a dog—with anything—or to hurt him by stepping on his feet, kneeing him in the chest, kicking him, or using a device such as a cattle prod. It sounds awful, but believe it or not, these are some of the ways people deal with aggression. Such actions are not only wrong, they're dangerous, and can easily make the problem worse.

What's the Prognosis?

How successful is treatment for aggression? It really depends a lot on how much of an effort you're willing to make. Treating aggression requires not only time but also the willingness to change your own behavior as well as your dog's. It also requires you to accept that your dog is always going to be at risk for aggressive behavior. There's no easy way around it: A dog who has a habit of biting can be made safer to be around, but there's no guarantee that he will never bite again. And treatment for ragelike behavior—described as unpredictable, impulsive, or sudden—is less likely to be successful.

Nonetheless, aggressive dogs can often be helped. By consistently ignoring unwanted behavior and rewarding good behavior, you can teach your dog how to live happily in the home, and the two of you can develop a mutually trusting relationship.

Obedience

Petiquette for Pooches

Some dogs wouldn't dream of challenging their people, while others are gunning for the top spot from the first day they walk into the house. It's important to know your dog and to establish yourself as her leader early on in the relationship. Not by being mean or bossy to the dog, but by being consistent in all your actions so she learns to work with and respect you.

The formal training of puppy kindergarten and obedience school are only one step toward teaching your dog to become a civilized member of the family. Classroom training is important, but it isn't enough to ensure that your dog becomes a successful member of human society.

In addition to classroom training, dogs need plenty of interaction with the world around them, a process known as socialization. Rewards, such as praise and treats, when they do the right thing (so they know to repeat those desirable behaviors); an understanding of their place in the family

pack; and—as with all lessons throughout life—practice, practice, practice are key in socializing your dog.

Because every human family is different, we all have different behaviors we want to teach our dogs. Nonetheless, the obedience lessons covered here will help your dog to be welcome both in your home and in public places.

Who's the Boss?

Teaching manners is important not only for harmonious living, but also to establish yourself as your dog's leader. When dogs live together they have a pack leader who decides when everyone eats and how much they get; where everyone sleeps; when playtime begins and ends; what kind of play will take place; what to investigate on the trail; and so on. Now that your dog lives with you, she needs you to be the pack leader and make those kinds of decisions for her. If you don't, she'll try to take over the

role of the pack leader herself, and that's not good.

Part of establishing leadership is teaching your dog to obey commands and how to behave in the house and around people. Be firm but not harsh. Avoid using discredited techniques such as alpha rolls—forcing the dog onto her back and staring at her—which are dangerous and ineffective. Instead, be consistent with what you ask of your dog and insist that she comply—as long as you're sure she understands what you want.

The Social Graces of the Urbane Dog

A happy, confident dog loves meeting people, plays well with other dogs, acts politely toward cats, and shows curiosity rather than fearfulness when encountering unfamiliar objects. When a dog has these attributes, she's said to be well socialized. A well-socialized dog isn't born, though; she's made. There's no doubt that a dog's

personality is important, but unless you make the effort to introduce Duchess to all kinds of people, places, and things at an early age, she will never reach her full social potential, and that would be a shame.

The critical period in a young pup's life is from three to fourteen weeks of age. That's when her brain is most open to new experiences. Older dogs benefit from socialization as well. It may take them a little longer to become accustomed to new things, but they can learn. Socialize them the same way you would a puppy. Remember, the most important factors that contribute to the making of a happy, confident dog are socialization and an understanding of her place within her human family.

For a well-adjusted dog, expose your pup in a positive way to people of all ages and appearances: people wearing hats or glasses; people on skateboards and bicycles; and people using

wheelchairs or walkers. Introduce her to the sounds of vacuum cleaners, lawn mowers, electronic toys, and any other noises she may commonly encounter.

Take Duchess to public places where dogs are welcome such as parks, pet supply stores, and—of course—the veterinary clinic and grooming shop. A lot of places permit well-behaved dogs, so keep it that way by taking your dog on leash and controlling her behavior in public.

Your attitude is the key to a confident dog. If Duchess sees that you're relaxed about a person's approach or a noise that's being made, she will follow your lead. Conversely, if she senses that you're anxious, she'll become anxious herself.

The veterinary clinic is a great place to start socializing your dog. Schedule an appointment for an exam or weight check only—no painful needles, please! Walk your dog into the clinic with a smile on your face, and let the staff greet her with pats and treats. If she seems fearful, don't try to soothe her by crooning that it's okay. That simply

confirms her belief that something awful awaits her. Just ignore her. Let her explore at her own pace; don't pick her up or force her toward staff members. Praise her when she investigates on her own, and ignore her if she's cowering under a chair. When Duchess is being brave or at least calm, praise her and give a treat. Repeat these just-for-fun vet visits as often as possible; there's no charge for bringing your dog to the clinic to be weighed and then giving her a treat.

Use this same technique anytime you take Duchess someplace new or introduce her to someone. Keep treats on hand so strangers can give one to Duchess when they meet. If your dog is reluctant to approach a new person, lay a trail of treats to him or her so Duchess can move toward the new person gradually—not to mention happily.

And remember—never force your dog to go toward someone: Fearful dogs bite! This advice applies to both large and small dogs. In fact, it's even more important for small dogs, because our first instinct is to pick them up and cuddle them.

Don't do it. Small dogs need to develop confidence just as much as large ones do—maybe even more so.

It's just as important for you to socialize Duchess with other dogs as it is for you to socialize her with other people. Training class is a great place for Duchess to meet other dogs. Some classes divide pups into groups of large and small dogs, but make sure your dog gets a chance to mix with dogs of all sizes and breeds. If she's big, she needs to learn to step carefully around small dogs, and if she's small she needs to learn to have confidence around her larger brethren.

Other good places to meet dogs are at parks. Plan a play date with friends and their dogs. Because parks are neutral terrain—they don't "belong" to any one dog—territorial disagreements are less likely to break out. Supervise the interactions until you're sure the dogs are getting along.

Beauty Is As Beauty Does

One of the signs of a nice dog is that she's willing to be petted or handled by many different people. This is important because it makes grooming, veterinary care, and participation in dog sports much easier. Willingness to be handled is a by-product of socialization. The dog who meets a lot of people learns to expect petting in a variety of situations. She learns that touch is pleasant, not frightening.

Start accustoming Duchess to being handled for grooming and veterinary care when she's a puppy. Take her in your lap and gently brush her. Speak softly to her, saying things such as "That feels

good, doesn't it, Duchess?" Lift up her ears and look inside them. Run your fingers around the inside of her lips. Stroke her paws and then pick them up and hold them. Although most dogs hate having their feet handled, they can learn to tolerate it if you start early enough and are persistent. A good time for these handling sessions is while you're watching TV.

At first, handle your dog for only a minute or two at a time, then gradually extend the length of time you spend grooming her. When she's used to having your fingers in her mouth, introduce her to a soft dog toothbrush. You'll be thankful for all of your prep work when her coat grows out and needs frequent combing or when she needs a bath.

Sitting Pretty

The *sit* command is one of the easiest to teach and one of the most useful. Pups can learn it at an early age, so it's a great way to accustom them to

the training process. Requiring your dog to sit is also a great way to reinforce your status as the leader.

The first thing Duchess should learn is that she gets attention when she sits. Not when she jumps up. Not when she runs away. When she sits. Because *sit* is often the first command dogs learn, it seems to stick more firmly in their brain, and they often respond to it more readily than to any other command. That's why it has so many great uses.

To teach the *sit* command, start by getting Duchess's attention. Show her a treat and slowly move it upward so she has to raise her head to see it. Most dogs naturally move into a sitting position when they do this. If Duchess isn't quite there, gently push down on her rump while moving your hand back over her head to give her the idea. When she's in position tell her to sit and give her the treat. Practice for only a couple of minutes (puppies have a short attention span) and repeat several times throughout the day. Soon Duchess will recognize that your uplifted hand signals the *sit* command even if you're not holding a treat.

Practice using the *sit* command in different situations once Duchess associates it with the action of sitting. Teach her to sit and wait before you pet her, before you feed her, and before you put her leash on. If you're out in the yard and she wanders away from you tell her to sit so she learns to respond even when you're at a distance. This won't be helpful if she's at risk of being hit by a car, but it can be useful in a more controlled situation when you simply want her to wait for you. (A leash, of course, is the best way to keep a dog under control and should always be used in unfamiliar or unfenced areas.)

To teach the *wait* or *stay* command, place your dog in a sit. Hold up your hand, with the flat of your palm toward the dog's face, and tell her to wait or stay (whichever you prefer); then back up a few steps. If your dog remains where she is, praise her. Gradually increase the amount of time she must wait before receiving praise or a reward. If she moves out of place, don't punish her, simply put her back in position and start over.

Jumping Up

Jumping is one of the most common complaints people have about their dogs. It may be cute when a puppy does it, but a couple of months later, when her size has doubled, it can become a problem. You don't want Duchess knocking down Aunt Mary or Baby Sue with her exuberant greeting. Replace jumping behavior as soon as possible with the *sit* command.

Teaching a dog not to jump up doesn't require any harsh tactics. Ignore anyone who tells you to

SIT.

knee the dog in the chest or push her away. Instead, simply pivot so she misses you. Then give the *sit* command. When she complies, give her a lot of praise or a treat. Repeat this every time she tries to jump up and insist that other people do so as well.

Often, especially with toy breeds, people say that they don't mind, and refuse to participate in the training process. If you have a large dog, that's not really an option because you don't want to run the risk of someone being injured, even inadvertently. It's not so bad with a toy breed, but remember that even small dogs can snag your stockings or scratch your legs when they jump up. It's better if you teach them the same good manners you would teach a larger dog.

On or Off the Furniture?

Lying on furniture or sleeping in bed is practically a given for the modern dog, but it should be a privilege rather than a right. Decide before you get a dog whether you want to allow her on the furniture at all or if you want to limit her to specific pieces of furniture or even to her own dog bed on the floor. In this matter there's no right or wrong decision, but it is one that you need to make and implement from day one so Duchess doesn't become confused.

The advantage to letting your dog on the furniture is that she's fun to snuggle with while you're reading or watching TV. Dogs are our best friends, after all. The disadvantage is that dogs leave hair and skin oils behind, which can make your furniture look shabby

in no time flat. If you want to cuddle with Duchess but still keep your sofa looking nice, you can compromise by covering it with a sheet or slipcover, or by laying down a blanket in a certain area and limiting your dog to that spot. You may also teach her that she's permitted only on certain pieces of furniture. For instance, the old sofa in the den is okay, but not the brocade one in the living room.

If you don't want Duchess on the furniture at all, never let her up on it—not even once. If she tries to get on the bed or sofa with you, take her to her bed or other designated area and tell her to stay. You will have to repeat this many times, but it will eventually sink in.

What about sleeping with you? A lot of trainers and behaviorists advise against this, saying that it gives the dog an overblown opinion of herself and can lead to problems with aggression. Again, because each dog is an individual, there is no right or wrong answer here. By establishing yourself as your dog's leader early on, she will learn to work with and respect you.

Mealtime Manners

Most dogs are highly motivated by food. When they know dinner's being prepared (yours or theirs), they may dance around, jump up on you, and otherwise get underfoot. While this is cute to watch (at least the first couple of times), it's not really the best behavior to permit in the kitchen, where you run the risk of stepping on Duchess or

dropping a hot pan because you tripped over her. Nor do you want a dog who practically snatches the food dish out of your hand as you're setting it down. The kitchen, then, is a great place for your dog to practice the *sit* command.

If you're preparing food, put your dog in a sit stay in an out-of-the-way corner. She can still watch; she just won't be in the way. As with any command, be consistent. You can't let your dog roam the kitchen sometimes and then expect her to understand why she's all of a sudden not allowed to.

Require your dog to sit before meals as well. This keeps her from jumping up and wolfing down her food. Because canine manners wither away if they're not used, this is a good way to get in a quick practice session twice a day.

Feed your dog before the rest of the family eats. Behaviorists now say that a well-fed dog is less likely to become anxious about guarding her food. She's also less likely to beg at the table, a bad habit that should be strongly discouraged. While the family eats, tell your dog to go to her place. Make sure the kids and your spouse don't slip her their veggies under the table; that only encourages begging behavior. Some dogs make a practice of lying beneath the baby's high chair, having learned that it's where manna falls from the heavens. Dogs are good vacuum cleaners, so you may not mind this if you have an especially messy baby, but be aware that it reinforces the begging habit. Decide now which is more important to you: a clean floor or a dog who doesn't beg.

Come When Called

Come is the most important command Duchess will ever learn. Use it to call her for meals, for playtime, for bedtime, and—most importantly—for taking her out of harm's way. When Duchess is about to run right in front of a speeding car and you scream at her to come and she responds instantly, you've just saved her life. If you don't teach your dog anything else, teach her to come when you call.

The *come* command is fun to teach because there's no way Duchess can mess it up. She's always going to get praise or a treat when she comes to

you. Start teaching the *come* command on the first day you bring your puppy or dog home. Puppies instinctively follow people. Use that instinct to your advantage. Make eye contact with your puppy and in your happiest, most excited tone of voice tell her to come. When she gets to you, make a big fuss and praise her.

Another way to get your dog excited about coming is to rattle a box of treats as you call her. Use something really good-smelling such as cat treats so she'll think it's worthwhile to head your way. Practice several times every day in different places. Anytime your dog heads toward you on her own, use it as a training opportunity. Tell her to come and praise and reward her when she gets to you.

Practice the *come* command when you're playing in the yard, holding Duchess's favorite toy. Instead of chasing Duchess, teach her to chase you. Hold treats or a toy and run away from her. As she takes off after you, tell her to come. When she catches you, praise her. Tell Duchess to come

when she follows you into the kitchen to prepare her meal. If you're a whistler, whistle a particular tune as you set down the food. If you can't whistle, try ringing a bell. Like Pavlov's dogs, Duchess will learn to come running every time she hears that melody.

Don't give the *come* command if you can't enforce it. Anytime Duchess doesn't come when you call, go and get her. Then walk her back to where you called her, telling her to come along the way and praising her when you get back to where you started.

Another way to do this is to practice the *come* command while your dog is wearing a leash. That way, if she doesn't come when you call, you can use the leash to enforce the command.

Never act angry when you're practicing the *come* command; you want Duchess to always be happy about coming to you. Never yell at your dog after she has come to you or call her and then do something unpleasant. If you need to give her a bath or trim her nails, go and get her.

No Marking Please!

Dogs are territorial animals, staking their claim to particular areas or objects in a variety of ways. One of these ways is urine-marking—Duke lifts his leg and squirts a shot of urine on the valued area. (Female dogs may also urine-mark and some even lift a leg to do so.) Most dogs do this outside on trees or light poles where it isn't a big deal, but sometimes they bring this behavior into the home where it's not acceptable at all. Your dog needs to learn that this is never permitted inside, not in your home and certainly not in anyone else's.

Urine-marks are usually found on vertical surfaces, such as the back of a sofa, a door, or a tall houseplant. Dogs who haven't been spayed or neutered are more likely to urine-mark, but altered dogs may take up the habit if they believe their territory is threatened.

The most common reasons dogs urine-mark include new animals in the home (your friend brings her dog over or you get a new puppy), conflicts with other animals in the home, unfamiliar objects in the dog's environment such as luggage or handbags belonging to visitors, and items that smell strange or have another animal's scent on them. All of these unfamiliar scents can trigger in your dog the need to assert that this is his place. Urine-marking in the house is a behavior problem rather than a house-training accident and should be dealt with accordingly.

What's the best way to handle urine-marking? If you don't plan to breed or show your dog, have

him or her neutered or spayed at or before sexual maturity (usually six to nine months of age, depending on the breed and the individual dog). Spaying and neutering can also help the problem in older animals, although it may take longer for them to break the habit of marking.

A bellyband on a male dog can also help prevent marking behavior. Bellybands are worn low on the dog's belly and cover the end of the penis so the dog can't mark. Your dog should wear a bellyband anytime you can't supervise him, or anytime he goes to someone's home or a public place such as a hotel.

If a bellyband isn't an option, make it unpleasant for your dog to mark. If he likes to lift his leg on the sofa or on a door, cover the area with aluminum foil. When the urine hits it, the sound will startle your dog, and the urine will probably splash back onto him.

Foil doesn't complement your decor? Take the initiative and put items your dog might mark out of his reach. Obviously, you can't do that with

furniture, so try changing the area so your dog won't want to mark there. Play with him or feed him in that area so he becomes comfortable.

Use an enzymatic cleanser to destroy the odor left by the urine. Avoid those with a strong fragrance; your dog may be tempted to mark over them. If you see your dog start to lift his leg or even sniff an area that he's marked previously, distract him by squeaking a toy or squirting him with a water gun. Reward him with praise if he abandons his plan to mark. When you can't be there to supervise, confine your dog outdoors in a securely fenced run, in a room where he doesn't mark, or in his crate. Prevention is the key to solving most behavior problems.

Is your dog unsure of himself because there's a new dog (cat, baby, spouse) in town? Help him make friends with the newcomer by recognizing and supporting the canine pecking order. Duke might have been top dog when it was just him, but now he needs to work out a relationship with the

new dog or person. Let it happen on the dog's terms. Just because your dog is older, bigger, or your favorite doesn't necessarily mean that he will automatically be the alpha dog. Oftentimes it's the little dogs who are in charge. Serious fights, however, indicate that a behaviorist's help is needed.

If the newcomer is a person, your dog needs to become familiar with him or her. A spouse or older child can take on the responsibility of feeding, grooming, or training him. A baby can't do that, but you can give Duke treats when he gently sniffs the baby or behaves calmly in his or her presence. In your dog's mind, Baby should equal Good Things.

Lastly, establish your own leadership. If Duke recognizes that you're in charge, he won't feel the need to mark territory. Avoid punishing your dog for urine-marking unless you catch him in the act. Instead, work to understand why he's marking so you can resolve the problem.

The Eleven Commandments of Good Dog Ownership

One of the best things you can have in life is a happy, successful relationship with your dog. To your dog, you are the leader she can always count on to keep her safe, fed, and cared for. To you, your dog is the best friend who always listens to

your problems and concerns. The following rules are your guide to forging this special friendship.

1. Train your dog. Be consistent and build on her strengths while understanding her limitations.

2. Never hit your dog or punish her after the fact.

3. Play with and exercise your dog every day.

4. Don't leave your dog alone for extended periods of time.

5. Feed your dog high-quality food and give her fresh water daily.

6. Supply clean and comfortable dog bedding for your dog's relaxation and sleep.

7. Never expose your dog to extreme heat or cold for long periods of time.

8. Pick up after your dog.

9. Provide your dog with regular veterinary care and grooming.

10. Never let your dog be a nuisance to the neighborhood by barking nonstop or roaming unsupervised.

11. Treat your dog as a beloved family member.

Index

A

accidents, avoiding house-training,
31–35, 35–39
active behavior modification, 171, 177
active breeds, 72
aggression
advice/help for, 166–168
appearance of aggressive dogs,
152–154
behavior modification for,
168–170, 171–177
definition of, 148–151
diet/exercise for dealing with,
180–181
drugs for, 178–180
success of treatment for, 183
territorial, 136
types of, 161–165
what not to do for, 182
aggressive breeds, 50
alpha dogs, 215–216. *See also* leadership by owners
American Veterinary Society of
Animal Behavior, 167
anxiety, 60, 74
barking due to, 129–131
chewing and, 43
digging due to, 97–99
medications for, 178–179
Applied Animal Behavior Society, 167
attention, withholding, 171–172

attention-seeking behavior, 93–96,
119, 132–134
avoidance of triggers, 170

B

baby gates, 54–55
barking
avoiding reinforcement of, 25–26
bark-control devices, 141–146
breeds known for, 119–121
encouraging appropriate,
138–139
general reasons for, 114–119
patience while correcting, 140–141
problem/inappropriate, 122–126,
126–138
puppy training, 147
to go out, 34
begging, 205–206
behavior modification
aggression, 168–170, 171–177
barking, 126–138, 140–141,
141–146
chewing, 68–74
consistency, 19, 28, 35, 205
digging, 98, 109–113
tools for, 174–175
bellybands, 213
black lights, 37
body language. *See also* communication

appearance of aggressive dogs,
    152–154
fear, 157
needing to go out, 12, 34
bones, types of, 57
breeds
    active, 72
    aggressive, 50
    difficult to house-train, 9–10
    digging, 80
    known for barking, 119–121
    scent hounds, 99–100
burying things, 102

C

chewing
    advice/help for problem, 73
    appropriate things to chew, 57–62
    dog-proofing to avoid, 50–56
    encouraging appropriate, 63–68
    general reasons for, 41–45
    preventing problems, 74–77
    problem/inappropriate, 45–49
    redirecting problem, 68–74
citronella collars, 107–108, 143–144
cleaning products, 35–39, 214
clicker training, 63–64
collars
    bark-control, 141–146
    citronella, 107–108
    electronic shock, 107–108
    for obedience training, 174–175
    sound-correction, 145
commandments of dog ownership,
    217–219

commands
    come, 207–210
    down, 75
    sit, 75, 196–199, 205
    stay/wait, 199
    teaching, 95
communication
    barking as, 114–119
    needing to go out, 12, 34
    of fear, 157
    through aggressive behavior, 149,
        152–154
confinement
    crating, 20–26, 71
    during house-training, 33
    of puppies, 54–56
conflict aggression, 155–156
consistency, 19, 28, 35, 205
correcting behaviors. *See* behavior
    modification; punishment to avoid
        counterconditioning, 176
crates, 71, 76
    for barking dogs, 131–132
    for house-training, 12, 14, 20–26
    for safety of puppies, 55–56
    misuse of, 24–25, 56

D

day care, 95–96
defensive behavior, 163–164
desensitization methods, 169–170, 176
diet, 180–181
digestive problems, 58–59
digging
    correcting the behavior, 109–113

for anxiety reduction, 97–99
for attention, 93–96
for escape, 99–101
for fun, 83–89
for prey, 89–91
for shelter, 91–93
general reasons for, 79–83
how to deter, 102–105
prevention methods, 101–103
digging breeds, 80
dog-proofing your house, 50–56
doghouses, 91–93, 131–132
down command, 75
drugs. *See* medications

E
electronic shock collars, 107–108, 142
encouraging behaviors, appropriate chewing, 63–68
escaping, digging for, 99–101
exercise, 72–73, 84–85, 128–129, 180–181

F
fear aggression, 157, 159, 162–163, 193
feeding
good nutrition, 180–181
in crates, 24
manners during, 204–206
schedules for, 29–30
fencing, 106, 108
formal training, 185–186
fun/playing

barking during, 135–136
digging for fun, 83–89
toys, 57–62, 64–67
furniture, keeping off, 201–203

G
gingivitis, 43
grooming, 195–196

H
handling your dog, 195–196
house-training
accidents during, 31–35
cleaning up accidents, 35–39
length of process, 8–12
paper-training, 15–19
problem prevention, 27–29
puppies, 12–15
rewarding for good performance, 19–20
secret to successful, 7–8
setting a schedule for, 29–30
using a crate, 20–26

I
intact (unneutered) males/females, 100–101, 211. *See also* spaying/neutering

J
jumping behavior, 200–201

L
leadership by owners, 75, 172–173, 185, 187–188, 197

learn to earn technique, 75
litter box training, 16, 18–19

M

manners. *See* obedience
maternal aggression, 162–163
mealtime manners, 204–206
medications
    for aggression, 168, 178–180
    for excessive barking, 131
    for separation anxiety, 98

N

neutering/spaying, 100–101, 151,
    211, 213
nuisance barking. *See* barking

O

obedience
    being the pack leader, 187–188
    coming when called, 207–210
    formal training, 185–186
    handling for, 195–196
    jumping behavior, stopping, 200–201
    keeping off furniture, 201–203
    mealtime manners, 204–206
    sit command, 196–199
    socialization and, 188–194
    training, 174–176
    urine-marking, stopping, 211–216
odor elimination, 35–39

P

pack leaders, owners as, 75,
    172–173, 187–188

pain-related aggression, 164–165, 166
paper-training, 15–19
passive behavior modification, 171,
    177
playing. *See* fun/playing
possessive aggressive, 161–162
predatory behavior/aggression, 89–91,
    159–160, 173–174
prevention methods
    chewing, 45–49, 68–74, 74–77
    digging, 101–103
    during house-training, 27–29
problems
    during house-training, 27–29
    excessive barking, 122–126,
        126–128
    inappropriate chewing, 45–49,
        68–74
    incorrect use of bark-control
        collars, 142
    misuse of crates, 24–25, 56
protective aggression, 158
punishment to avoid. *See also*
    behavior modification
    alpha rolls, 188
    during house-training, 32
    for aggression, 155, 168, 182
    for barking, 126
    harsh methods, 112
    kneeing in the chest, 201
    scolding, 15, 70
    using crates as, 25
puppies
    barking of, 119
    bladder control of, 9

body language of, 153–154
confining, 33
house-training, 12–15
preschool for, 147, 158
problem barking in, 147
socialization of, 189–190
teething, 41–42

R
rawhide bones, 58–59
rewards
    during house-training, 19–20
    encouraging appropriate barking,
        138–139
    for calm behavior, 172
    for crating, 23–24
    for good potty behavior, 27–28
    for not barking, 123–126
    positive reinforcement, 67–68
    praise, 12, 28
    unintentional, 125–126
rules for good ownership, 218–219
runs, outdoor, 90–91

S
safety issues
    biting/aggression, 166, 183, 193
    dog-proofing your house, 50–56
    electrical cords, 53
    ingesting objects, 46
    muzzling, 124–125
    of bark-correction collars, 146
    pesticides, 90
    rawhide bones, 58–59
scent hounds, 99–100
schedules, house-training, 10, 29–30

scolding, 15, 70, 76
separation anxiety, 43, 60, 74,
    97–98
shelter, digging for, 91–93
sit command, 75, 196–199, 205
socialization, 185–186, 188–194
sound-correction collars, 145
spaying/neutering, 100–101, 151,
    211, 213
stain removal, 35–39
stay command, 199
stress, 46. *See also* anxiety

T
teething, 41–42
territorial behavior/aggression,
    157–158, 176–177, 211–216
toys, 75, 86, 126–127
training. *See also* house-training
    clicker, 63–64
    formal, 185–186
    obedience, 85, 94
    patience during, 140–141
    playing with toys, 64–68
treats, 61, 192–193. *See also* rewards

U
urine-marking, 157, 211–216

V
veterinary visits, 191–192

W
wait command, 199
watchdogs, 138–139